Bankruptcy Risk in Financial Depository Intermediaries

Arthur D. Little Books

A series of books on management and other scientific and technical subjects by senior professional staff members of Arthur D. Little, Inc., the international consulting and research organization. The series also includes selected nonproprietary case studies.

Acquisition and Corporate Development
    James W. Bradley and Donald H. Korn

Bankruptcy Risk in Financial Depository Intermediaries: Assessing Regulatory Effects
    Michael F. Koehn

Board Compass: What It Means to Be a Director in a Changing World
    Robert Kirk Mueller

Career Conflict: Management's Inelegant Dysfunction
    Robert Kirk Mueller

The Corporate Development Process
    Anthony J. Marolda

Corporate Responsibilities and Opportunities to 1990
    Ellen T. Curtiss and Philip A. Untersee

Modeling Industry-Location Dynamics: Microeconometric Modeling for Policy Analysis
    Kirkor Bozdogan and David Wheeler

System Methods for Socioeconomic and Environmental Impact Analysis
    Glenn R. De Souza

Bankruptcy Risk in Financial Depository Intermediaries

Assessing Regulatory Effects

Michael F. Koehn

An Arthur D. Little Book

LexingtonBooks
D.C. Heath and Company
Lexington, Massachusetts
Toronto

LIBRARY
The University of Texas
At San Antonio

Library of Congress Cataloging in Publication Data

Koehn, Michael F.
  Bankruptcy risk in financial depository intermediaries.

  (Arthur D. Little series)
  Bibliography: p.
  Includes index.
  1. Banking law—United States. 2. Bankruptcy—United States. 3. Bank failures—United States.
  I. Title.
  KF974.K63   346'.73'078   79-2411
  ISBN 0-669-03169-0

Published simultaneously in Canada.

Printed in the United States of America.

International Standard Book Number: 0-669-03169-0

Library of Congress Catalog Card Number: 79-2411

Contents

List of Figures

List of Tables

Acknowledgments

While space does not permit individual recognition of all those who were instrumental in the completion of this study, I wish to express my appreciation for their assistance. There are, however, several individuals who should be singled out for their considerable efforts.

I owe a special debt of gratitude to Professors Mark J. Flannery, Richard C. Marston, and Monique G. Spielberg who reviewed carefully early drafts of the manuscript and offered many suggestions for improvement. Special thanks are due to Professor Anthony M. Santomero, who provided invaluable guidance, suggestions, and comments as the study progressed. Of course, I alone am responsible for the form in which my work now appears, and for whatever misuse I might have made of their suggestions.

While revising subsequent drafts of the manuscript, I benefited greatly from the comments of my colleagues and corporate clients. In particular, the comments and assistance provided by Lawrence Lapide, Helen Ojha, and Bruce Stangle were quite helpful. Roberta Green, Patricia LeBlanc, and Patricia Smith carried the burden of typing numerous revisions and drafting the original set of figures. My wife Stacy devoted much of her free time to editing early drafts of the manuscripts. I am also indebted to the Operations Research Section at Arthur D. Little, Inc., which provided me time to complete this study.

1 Introduction

Depository intermediaries operate within an environment dominated by laws and regulations. These laws and regulations, ranging from limitations on branching to restrictions on portfolios, strongly influence the activities of depository intermediaries. While responding to broad issues of monetary policy, the primary objective of these regulations is to maintain institutional soundness and solvency. The ultimate goal of these regulations is to protect depositors and the depository system as a whole and therefore the health of the economy.[1]

The extensive regulation of financial intermediaries reflects the critical role that this sector plays in the savings and investment process. A stable and solvent financial system is indeed necessary to permit an efficient allocation of resources that is crucial to the health of the general economy. The rationale for these regulations rests on the notion that the interests of the whole economy must be considered in conjunction with the interests peculiar to financial intermediaries.

In its fundamentals, the regulation of financial intermediaries claims to supplement the competitive market that is otherwise incapable of promoting a sound financial system. It further claims that the benefits of a competitive financial industry cannot outweigh its potential for disruption in the economy as a whole. This risk stems from the role of financial intermediaries as custodians of the nation's credit and payments networks, which includes a fiduciary responsibility for significant capital resources. Disruptions of continuity in the fiduciary function create the potential for unacceptable disturbance of these networks. Such disturbances could result in a collapse of the depositors' confidence in the banking system.[2]

Solvency Regulations

There are myriad laws and regulations designed explicitly to protect and preserve the solvency of depository intermediaries. These laws and regulations can be summarized under three major regulatory instruments: portfolio restrictions, capital adequacy requirements, and Regulation Q restrictions. Each of these major instruments of regulation is designed to affect the operating behavior of depository intermediaries thereby promoting the soundness of financial institutions and the intermediary system. However, these instruments may in fact increase the risk of an intermediary and promote excessive risk taking. The conflicting effects of each regulatory instrument are as follows.

Portfolio Restrictions

It is generally argued that the primary benefit derived from limiting the composition of the asset portfolio (for example, limiting the quantity or proportion of funds that may be allocated to a particular asset) is to restrict institutions from making too risky loans or from purchasing notes/securities of marginal borrowers. Presumably, these restrictions protect the capital of an intermediary by reducing risk exposure and therefore the probability of failure. [Note that these restrictions are also designed to act as credit-allocation devices, for example, mortgage quantity requirements imposed on savings-and-loan institutions (S&Ls).] [3]

However, asset restrictions may on balance have the perverse effect of generating an unstable financial environment—a situation contrary to the objectives of the regulations. For example, limiting the investment opportunity set of an intermediary reduces the possibilities the firm has to diversify its portfolio. The inability of an institution to diversify away some risk may actually result in a higher risk exposure and a higher probability of failure.

Indeed, because asset restrictions reduce portfolio diversification possibilities, depository intermediaries may be unable to reduce or eliminate diversifiable risk and therefore unable to hold a less risky portfolio. Intermediaries are therefore faced with a risk-return trade-off that may be unfavorable relative to an unconstrained situation; every point on their investment-possibilities frontier may be worse or less efficient than the unconstrained frontier (that is, the expected return for any given level of risk is lower). Consequently, these constraints may result in less efficient use of an intermediary's available funds and higher deposit risk.

At best the net effect of asset restrictions on total risk is not clear. In cases where the excluded assets would significantly add risk (defined either in terms of default, market, or interest-rate risk) to the portfolio, this type of regulation may reduce failure exposure. On the other hand, if the excluded assets substantially reduce residual risk, the effect will be a higher chance of insolvency. [4]

Restrictions placed on the portfolio may also exacerbate the total risk of intermediaries during periods of rising interest rates. For example, portfolios composed of short-term assets (for example, consumer loans) are not subject to the same degree of interest-rate risk as those portfolios made up of long-term mortgages. Savings-and-loan institutions, which are required to hold a large quantity of mortgages in their portfolios, are therefore particularly vulnerable during these periods. In other words, an increase in the expected cost of funds (deposits), combined with a portfolio composed of low-interest-paying mortgages transacted during periods of low interest rates, implies a reduction in profitability for S&Ls. In fact, a negative interest-rate spread may occur with a corresponding increase in the probability of insolvency. [5]

Reserve requirements are analogous to other asset restrictions in several respects. First, reserve requirements reduce liquidity by forcing an intermediary to hold assets in a form that cannot be readily converted to available cash. Second, required reserves reduce the income an intermediary may earn on its total capital stock, which in turn may influence it to shift into riskier loan/securities to offset the loss of income.[6]

Finally, reserves may induce institutions to discriminate against particular loan-liability structures, which may lead to less financial services provided to particular segments of the market. For example, because the marginal cost of demand deposits increases relative to the cost of certificates of deposits when reserve requirements are considered, intermediaries may discriminate against small consumers. It appears, therefore, that asset restrictions including reserve requirements work to reduce institutional soundness and profitability.[7]

Capital Adequacy Requirements

The capitalization of depository intermediaries is at least implicitly regulated. Typically, rules of thumb such as a capital-asset ratio or capital-risk-asset ratio are used to measure and compare the capital adequacy of these institutions.[8] These capital standards are imposed to ensure that adequate surplus exists to protect depositors from losing their funds under most conditions. Capital standards are therefore designed to reduce the probability of insolvency. The higher the capitalization, other things being equal, the less risk depositors must assume.

However, high capital standards limit the leverage capacity and therefore the potential for high returns of a depository intermediary. Low returns on capital, induced by these standards, may subsequently create difficulties for these institutions in attracting new capital, which in turn will restrict the supply of credit required to sustain growth in real investment. Moreover, a depository intermediary may reshuffle its asset portfolio toward riskier securities to offset the loss of income caused by high capital standards.[9] This behavior may in the long run adversely affect the depositor.

With regard to capital adequacy requirements, the crucial question arises of whether the capital of depository intermediaries should be regulated at all. It is often argued that the capital markets should be permitted to determine the capital structure of intermediaries. If the capital of an intermediary is too low, the market will perceive the firm as being too risky. The market value of the firm's equity will drop, thereby raising the firm's cost of capital until the intermediary has reduced its scale, or, in other words, until the capital-asset ratio has risen. The market mechanism will therefore regulate in this manner to ensure the appropriate capitalization of the firm given the riskiness of its portfolio and environment.[10]

The problem with having the capital markets regulate capital adequacy is one of social cost. It is well known that competitive market pricing mechanisms fail to consider the broad externalities that may exist with any given service or institution. The capital market cannot therefore be completely trusted to determine proper capital requirements, and some form of capital regulation is indeed required.[11]

Regulation Q Restrictions

Regulation Q restrictions are designed to provide intermediaries with access to deposit funds at interest rates that are on average below those prevailing in the competitive capital markets. Regulators argue that these "cheap" deposit liabilities result in making these institutions safer by preventing destructive competition for funds among depository intermediaries and by ensuring that an intermediary can earn a positive interest rate spread over almost any level of interest rates. This in turn ensures that the firm can earn a positive return on capital. By implication then, an intermediary need not invest in excessively risky securities to earn a reasonable return on capital, since such a return is for the most part ensured. [Note that the marginal cost of deposits may be greater than the Regulation Q ceilings since the rates paid on large certificates of deposit (CDs) are not regulated. However, the average cost of total deposit liabilities will be lower as a result of deposit-rate ceilings.]

However, opponents to this regulation argue that intermediaries can and do circumvent Regulation Q rate ceilings to attract and compete for funds by using inefficient, non-interest-paying devices such as advertising or gifts to depositors.[12] They further argue that although Regulation Q restrictions may reduce the average cost of funds, and in turn the probability of insolvency of banks and other depository intermediaries, legislative repeal of Regulation Q would result in a more efficient allocation of capital funds as depositors receive the real interest-rate benefits generated from their deposits. Moreover, repeal of Regulation Q would lead to less disintermediation activity since depository intermediaries would be able to compete freely in the capital markets for funds.

Examination of the average cost of funds to financial depository intermediaries reveals that Regulation Q restrictions have not been fully circumvented.[13] Intermediaries still enjoy access to deposit funds at interest rates that are on average lower than what would prevail in the competitive capital markets. In light of this effect of Regulation Q, it appears that elimination of these ceilings would raise the average cost of funds for depository institutions. An increase in cost would reduce earnings that may raise risk exposure if depository intermediaries attempt to offset the higher priced funds. (Note that repeal of deposit-rate ceilings would increase risk exposure even if intermediaries did not reshuffle the composition of their portfolio. As earnings fall, fewer dollars are available to protect against unexpected loan default.) This in turn would lead to higher average loan rates. Perhaps small depositors would initially benefit from repeal of Regulation Q, but institutional failures may result as earnings fall.[14]

Purpose of the Study

As suggested previously, the expressed goal of solvency regulation is to protect the depositor and to ensure the solidity of the depository intermediary system. This stated goal is sound, but several instruments of solvency regulation may produce unintended effects that result in increasing rather than decreasing overall risk and the chance of insolvency. It thus appears that the public, whose interest the regulator is charged with protecting, may indeed be penalized in that the chance of system failure is greater.

The purpose of this study is to investigate the effects that solvency regulations (that is, asset restrictions, capital adequacy restraints, and Regulation Q restrictions) have on an intermediary's investment opportunity set, its quality of earnings, and its probability of bankruptcy. The central focus is to determine whether the goal of deposit safety and institutional soundness is actually achieved or rather if regulation results in a reduction of earnings and an increase in the probability of failure for regulated depository intermediaries.

Each solvency instrument will be examined individually to determine how it affects earnings and the probability of insolvency. In addition, the interrelationships among the broad solvency instruments will be analyzed to determine their simultaneous impact on the single-period risk-return opportunity locus of the firm (that is, the attributes of the probability distribution of rates of return to invested capital) and the probability of failure.[15]

The purpose of this study is not only to examine the impacts of solvency restrictions on a depository intermediary in general but also to examine and compare the relative effects of these restrictions across each type of depository intermediary. These institutions are commercial banks, mutual savings banks, S&Ls, and credit unions.

Outline of the Study

This study presents an accounting of the effects of solvency constraints and regulations on depository intermediary risk and the probability of insolvency. As mentioned earlier, this investigation will be carried out for each of the four major types of depository intermediaries. The analysis proceeds in the following steps.

Chapter 2 characterizes and describes each financial depository intermediary in terms of its particular portfolio restrictions, reserve requirements, Regulation

Q restrictions, and capital requirements. The regulatory agencies that supervise each depository intermediary are identified and discussed briefly.

Chapter 3 presents a simple, single-period financial model of an intermediary. Although this is a partial equilibrium model, it does permit us to isolate the unique effects of each solvency regulation and to identify the overall effect of these regulations operating simultaneously. Thus with the aid of this model, we examine each solvency regulation with respect to its effect on the firm's profitability and on several parameters of the probability distributions of rates of return on invested capital (that is, the risk-return opportunity locus facing invested capital). The initial focus of this chapter is to investigate the effects of asset restrictions and Regulation Q restrictions. Leverage constraints or capital adequacy regulations are subsequently analyzed. Finally, the interrelationship between the existence of depository intermediaries and solvency regulations is examined.

Chapter 4 describes the data used for an empirical examination of the effects of solvency regulation. Several parameters of the distributions of ex-post rates of return for various assets such as common stocks, government bonds, corporate bonds, mortgages, commercial-bank loans, and consumer loans are presented. These data are used in chapter 5 to simulate the risk-return possibilities over various sets of financial assets. In addition, loan losses are estimated. These data are needed to provide an estimate of the ex-ante default rate for each loan category (see appendix B). Finally, the estimates of the effective standards of solvency regulation for each type of depository institution are reported.

Chapter 5 presents the empirical findings of the effects of solvency constraints. In general, these findings provide approximations of the effect each constraint has on each type of intermediary. First, the effect that asset restrictions have on each intermediary's investment frontier is reported. Second, a risk-free asset is introduced, and the simulated investment opportunity locus of each intermediary is presented. Third, Regulation Q ceilings are introduced, and the risk-return opportunity locus is then estimated. Given these estimates, the relative effect on earnings is compared across each type of intermediary. Finally, a sensitivity analysis of leverage, risk, and rate of return on invested capital to changes in reserve requirements, asset restrictions, and deposit-rate ceilings is presented.

Chapter 6 examines the effects that solvency regulations have on the probability of bankruptcy. Recall that regulation is based on some notion of bank soundness and the resulting probability of failure. Thus the total portfolio risk as well as the relative positions of the efficient frontier must be related analytically to the probability of failure. The impacts of each type of restriction can then be compared in terms of this probability. The result will provide some indication of the cost and effectiveness of each type of solvency restriction leading to an identification of those restrictions that most adversely affect a depository intermediary. To carry out this analysis, a single-period measure of the probability of failure is presented.[16] Subsequently, the sensitivity of bankruptcy probabilities to changes in several solvency constraints is examined and the findings are reported.

Brief Summary of Results

Our results demonstrate that each solvency instrument indeed produces several undesirable effects. Specifically, portfolio restrictions increase the probability of bankruptcy. In general, asset restrictions do not permit the recognition that a large number of available assets lead to a reduction of risk through diversification of the portfolio. Deposit-rate ceilings, on the other hand, permit favorable borrowing rates for an intermediary. As a result, this regulation appears to protect the firm from insolvency even though the variance of the cost of funds may increase under deposit-rate ceilings relative to an unconstrained regime. Finally, capital regulation serves to protect depositors from the loss of funds by constraining an intermediary from operating within the high-risk areas of its opportunity set. However, if the firm is unable to offset the effects of asset restrictions, it may not provide the return required by its owners.

The net effect of these regulations appears to reduce profitability, increase total risk, and increase the probability of failure of a depository intermediary relative to the unconstrained regime. If this overall effect is significant, then the industry will have difficulty raising capital to support any level of deposits. This in turn will reduce the quantity of funds available for real investment, and the growth of the real economy may suffer.

Although asset restrictions were found to lower the risk-return locus of all types of intermediaries, S&Ls and mutual savings banks were found to be most severely affected by these regulations. Deposit-rate ceilings, on balance, raise the risk-return locus of each intermediary; however, for S&Ls and mutual savings banks, this positive effect does not appear to be strong enough to offset the negative effects of asset restrictions. Reserve requirements, on the other hand, reduce the profitability of each intermediary but not to the extent that asset restrictions do. Finally, leverage constraints restrict the operating area of a credit union to a much greater extent than for other intermediaries.

The analysis shows that the relative ranking of risk-return loci and risk of insolvency are identical. In general, commercial banks and credit unions enjoy the most favorable set of solvency regulations in that their risk-return loci approximate the locus of an unconstrained intermediary. Accordingly, the risk of insolvency is lowest for commercial banks and credit unions and highest for mutual savings banks and S&Ls. It appears therefore that commercial banks and credit unions have been provided a competitive advantage in the market for investors and depositors as a result of the differential in regulatory standards across types of intermediaries.

Even though the short portfolio horizon used in this study may bias the empirical results toward commercial banks and credit unions, the results reported appear to be indicative of the general effects of solvency regulation. Asset restrictions adversely affect the probability of default. Regulation Q ceilings protect an intermediary, but they could be removed safely if asset restrictions were also eliminated. Reserve requirements also increase the probability of insolvency yet their impact is small relative to asset restrictions. Finally, leverage constraints have only a negligible effect on the probability of failure relative to the unconstrained regime.

Notes

1. For an in-depth discussion of the objectives of commercial-bank regulation, see D. Jacobs, "The Framework of Commercial Bank Regulation: An Appraisal," in *Innovations in Bank Management,* ed. P.F. Jessup (New York: Holt, Rinehart and Winston, 1969), pp. 831-846. For a discussion of this issue and Federal Deposit Insurance Corporation (FDIC) insurance reform, see K. Scott and T. Mayer, "Risk and Regulation in Banking: Some Proposals for Federal Deposit Insurance Reform," *Stanford Law Review* 23 (1971):857-902. The claim that ensuring the safety of the financial system is the primary objective of regulation is not to deny that regulators also care about the competitive structure of the industry, only that the competitive structure of the industry is of secondary importance relative to the solidity of the system.

2. See J.M. Guttentag, "Reflections on Bank Regulatory Structure and Large Bank Failures," in *Conference on Bank Structure and Competition* (Chicago: Federal Reserve Bank of Chicago, 1975), pp. 136-149, for a discussion of the impact of large bank failures on the depository intermediary system.

3. As we mentioned in the text, not all portfolio restrictions are designed to protect the solvency of an intermediary. Nonetheless, these restrictions may generate unwanted effects with respect to the safety of the firm. Accordingly, we will treat all portfolio restrictions as if their primary goal was the solvency of an intermediary.

4. As we discuss in more detail later, whether an asset contributes significant risk to an intermediary's portfolio depends on how its returns covary with the returns of the other assets included in the portfolio. Clearly, without analyzing these properties for each restricted asset, regulators cannot know a priori which assets contribute significant risk and therefore should be excluded from the investment opportunity set of intermediaries.

5. In other words, due to portfolio restrictions, the firm is unable to hedge against a shift in the yield curve.

6. The effects of reserves on the liquidity and portfolio behavior of depository intermediaries has been discussed extensively in the literature. See,

for example, J. Ascheim, "Open Market Operations Versus Reserve Requirement Variations," *Economic Journal* 69 (1959):697-704; and C.J. Prestopiio, "The Impact of Differential Reserve Requirements on Commercial Bank Liquidity and Portfolio Management," Ph.D. dissertation, University of Pennsylvania, 1974. Also see appendix A.

7. Before proceeding, we should mention that because asset restrictions artificially separate or segment the financial markets, the allocation of capital in the economy may also be unfavorably affected. For example, if S&Ls are required to invest all their funds in mortgages, then the rate of return per unit of risk offered in this market may diverge from that offered in other markets. As a result, the risk-adjusted marginal rate of return on all assets will diverge leading to suboptimal investments and social loss. Clearly, if intermediaries are not permitted to operate in all financial asset markets, then the arbitrage mechanism that would work to bring equality of the marginal rates of return across all markets is either weakened or eliminated. Equally important, intermediaries that are permitted to operate in nearly all asset markets will most likely enjoy a favorable risk-return opportunity locus relative to those intermediaries that are more severely constrained. This effect translates into an advantage for these institutions in that they can more readily attract and retain capital.

8. For a discussion and description of the capital adequacy ratios used by regulatory authorities, see Reed et al., *Commercial Banking* (Englewood Cliffs, N.J.: Prentice-Hall, 1976), pp. 402-420.

9. See M.F. Koehn and A.M. Santomero, "Regulation of Bank Capital and Portfolio Risk," mimeographed (Philadelphia, Penn.: University of Pennsylvania, 1978). They show under plausible assumptions that commercial banks may more than offset an increase in required capital by shifting to riskier securities.

10. Several authors have argued that the capital markets should regulate the capital adequacy of depository intermediaries. For example, see J. Pringle, "The Capital Decision in Commercial Banks," *Journal of Finance* 24 (1974):779-796; or G. Vojta, *Bank Capital Adequacy* (New York: Citicorp, 1973). For a different view, see A.M. Santomero and R. Watson, "Determining the Optimal Capital Standards for the Banking Industry," *Journal of Finance* 32 (1977):1267-1282. We should note that prior to single and multiple bank holding companies, the current capital restrictions constrained investors from revising the capital structure of a bank to a structure that might be perceived as "optimal."

11. As a result of the critical role depository intermediaries play in the payments mechanism, failure of a depository intermediary not only affects the equity holder but also users of the payments mechanism (which of course includes depositors). Failure therefore causes external effects that are not adequately captured in the pricing mechanism of the competitive capital markets. As a result, some form of regulation is required to protect depositors and users of the payments mechanism from the external effects of intermediary failure. For a discussion of the effect of externalities on the pricing mechanism

of a competitive market, see E. Malinvaud, *Lectures on Microeconomic Theory* (Amsterdam: North-Holland Publishing, 1972), pp. 200-211.

12. See R. Barro and A.M. Santomero, "Household Money Holdings and the Demand Deposit Rate," *Journal of Money, Credit, and Banking* 4 (1972):397-413, for a discussion of this issue.

13. See R. Startz, "Implicit Interest on Demand Deposits," *Journal of Monetary Economics,* in press.

14. For an excellent summary of the literature dealing with the costs and benefits of Regulation Q rate ceilings and the possible impact if these ceilings are either eliminated or changed, see J. Mingo, "Deposit-rate Ceilings: Microeconomic Considerations," in *Evaluation of the Social Impact of Regulation of Consumer Financial Services,* a Preliminary Report to the National Science Foundation prepared by Abt Associates (Cambridge: Abt Associates, 1977), pp. 578-612.

15. It is important to recognize that the effects of solvency regulations are primarily of an intraperiod nature. Consequently, a single-period model is quite adequate for the issues being investigated. It is also important to note that in order to assess the claim of regulation that it protects and enhances the solidity of the depository intermediary system, we must analyze the effects that regulation has on both the risk and return characteristics of the firm.

16. The measure of the probability of failure comes from A. Roy, "Safety First and the Holding of Assets," *Econometrica* 20 (1952):431-449. Using Roy's model, R. Blair and A. Heggestad, "Bank Portfolio Regulation and the Probability of Bank Failure," *Journal of Money, Credit, and Banking* 10 (1978):88-93, have examined bank portfolio restrictions and their impact on insolvency. This study exploits this relationship for the purposes of examining the full range of solvency regulation on the probability of failure (see chapter 6).

2 Depository Intermediaries and Their Solvency Constraints

Regulatory instruments designed to ensure solvency contain standards unique to each type of depository intermediary. The relative effects of solvency regulations across depository intermediaries are importantly determined by these differing standards. Before proceeding to the analysis of these effects, an overview of financial institutions is provided, and each type of depository intermediary is characterized along with its respective standards.

Overview

Depository intermediaries play an important role in the growth and development of the economy. By their very nature, these institutions reconcile or "intermediate" the conflicting objectives of primary borrowers and lenders.

The assets of depository intermediaries are composed chiefly of financial claims representing obligations of primary borrowers. These primary obligations may be risk-free, of short maturity, and highly marketable or highly risky, of long maturity, and relatively illiquid due to a thin secondary market for these securities.

The liabilities of depository intermediaries are composed for the most part of contractual obligations representing claims of depositors. These deposits are the major source of funds for these institutions. Accordingly, the net worth, or reserve position, is minor relative to total assets; that is, permanent capital is a relatively insignificant source of funds.

To illustrate the importance of depository intermediaries in the functioning of the economy, tables 2-1 and 2-2 present data on the supply and demand for credit in the United States and the share of credit supplied by these institutions. As the tables indicate, depository institutions have grown increasingly more important as sources of all types of credit. From 1961 to 1965, depository intermediaries supplied approximately 62 percent of all credit advanced. From 1971 to 1975, these same institutions supplied approximately 70 percent of all credit advanced.

The importance of depository institutions is further indicated in table 2-3, which presents the assets of financial institutions from 1960 to 1975. In this

Table 2-1
Summary of Supply and Demand for Credit
($ Billions)

	Annual Net Increases in Amounts Outstanding							Amounts Outstanding 12/31/77(e)
	1972	1973	1974	1975	1976	1977(e)	1978(p)	
Net Demand for Credit								
Privately held mortgages	68.8	68.7	42.8	40.2	72.0	94.0	97.0	866.4
Corporate bonds	18.9	13.2	26.9	32.9	30.7	29.5	32.2	366.2
Domestically held foreign bonds	1.0	1.0	2.2	6.2	8.4	4.3	4.0	37.5
Long-term private	88.7	82.9	71.9	79.3	111.1	127.8	133.2	1,270.1
Business loans	26.2	41.0	35.6	-12.4	5.4	34.1	43.5	277.0
Consumer installment credit	14.8	21.4	9.3	7.5	20.5	32.0	36.5	217.5
All other bank loans	9.4	6.8	3.6	2.7	12.1	13.2	14.0	114.3
Open-market paper	1.6	8.3	17.7	-1.3	8.1	13.7	15.5	88.2
Short-term private	52.0	77.5	66.2	-3.5	46.1	93.0	109.5	697.0
Privately held treasury debt	16.0	-0.6	9.7	76.3	58.6	48.2	54.2	453.8
Privately held federal agency debt	11.5	22.2	19.7	11.5	16.9	24.4	30.0	163.5
Subtotal federal	27.5	21.6	29.4	87.8	75.5	72.6	84.2	617.3
State and local tax-exempt bonds	14.1	13.3	11.9	17.5	21.7	30.4	23.2	260.9
State and local tax-exempt notes	-1.3	0.8	2.6	-1.2	-4.6	-0.7	-2.0	12.6
Tax-exempt	12.8	14.1	14.5	16.3	17.1	29.7	21.2	273.5
Total net demand for credit	181.0	196.1	182.0	179.9	249.8	323.1	348.1	2,857.9
Net Supply of Credit[a]								
Mutual savings banks	8.8	5.3	3.2	10.6	12.5	11.8	10.8	134.5
S/Ls	35.3	27.1	19.6	37.4	50.5	60.5	57.4	410.8
Credit unions	3.0	3.6	2.8	5.4	5.8	7.5	7.6	45.1
Life insurance companies	8.8	10.0	10.3	15.3	22.3	23.6	24.2	256.1

Fire and casualty companies	3.8	3.5	4.6	8.2	8.8	10.5	11.0	74.3
Private noninsured pension funds	-0.7	2.0	5.8	7.9	5.3	10.2	11.4	67.0
State and local retirement funds	3.1	3.4	8.0	8.3	9.6	10.9	11.2	95.1
Foundations and endowments	-0.1	0.6	0.9	1.1	0.9	0.7	1.0	16.8
Closed-end corporate bond funds	1.2	1.1	0.2	0.0	0.0	0.0	0.0	2.8
Money market funds	0.0	0.0	1.0	0.7	0.4	-0.3	0.5	1.9
Municipal bond funds	0.4	0.7	1.1	2.2	3.1	4.5	5.0	13.8
Open-end taxable investment funds	0.0	-0.2	-0.4	0.8	1.1	1.1	0.3	9.6
Real estate investment trusts	4.1	5.6	0.2	-4.9	-3.7	-1.5	-1.2	7.8
Finance companies	9.4	11.6	4.9	1.3	8.7	19.9	20.0	122.5
Total nonbank institutions	77.1	74.3	62.2	94.3	125.3	159.4	159.2	1,258.1
Commercial banks[b]	73.3	77.6	59.8	31.0	64.0	78.4	93.3	883.8
Business corporations	-2.7	0.9	8.8	9.5	11.9	7.7	5.3	74.3
State and local governments	5.5	3.3	1.2	3.4	4.9	15.5	13.1	58.7
Foreigners	8.4	0.6	11.2	6.1	15.2	30.2	31.8	126.9
Subtotal	161.6	156.7	143.2	144.3	221.3	291.2	302.7	2,401.8
Residual households direct	19.4	39.4	38.8	35.6	28.5	31.9	45.4	456.1
Total Net Supply of Credit	181.0	196.1	182.0	179.9	249.8	323.1	348.1	2,857.9

Source: Salomon Brothers, *Prospect for the Credit Markets in 1978* (New York: Salomon Brothers, 1977). Reprinted with permission.

Note: e = estimated; p = preliminary.

[a]Excludes funds for equities, cash, and miscellaneous demands not tabulated above.

[b]Includes loans transferred to books of nonoperating holding and other bank-related companies.

Table 2-2
Importance of Financial Institutions as a Source of Credit

	Credit Advanced (Annual Average, $ Billions)			Annual Growth in Annual Average (%)
	1961-1965	1966-1970	1971-1975	1961-1975
Depository Institutions				
Commercial banks	20.5	27.4	57.5	7.64
S&Ls	10.7	8.9	29.2	7.43
Mutual savings banks	3.4	4.0	7.9	6.20
Credit unions	0.7	1.4	3.4	12.00
Total	35.3	41.7	98.0	7.57
Nondepository Institutions				
Finance companies	3.4	3.9	6.5	4.74
Security brokers and dealers	0.3	0.9	(0.1)	–
Life insurance companies	6.9	8.6	15.0	5.70
Fire and casualty insurance companies	1.2	2.9	5.2	11.04
Mutual funds	1.4	2.3	(1.0)	–
Noninsured pension funds	8.2	11.1	17.5	5.56
Total	21.4	29.7	42.8	5.43
Total, all categories	56.7	71.4	140.8	6.71

Source: Board of Governors of the Federal Reserve System, Flow-of-Funds Accounts 1946-1975 (1976), pp. 79-80.

table, the financial assets of depository institutions are compared to those of nondepository financial institutions. Nondepository financial institutions include life insurance companies, noninsured pension funds, finance companies, fire and casualty insurance companies, mutual funds, and security brokers and dealers. As the table indicates, over the period 1960 to 1975 the financial assets of depository institutions grew at an annual rate of 9.4 percent, whereas the assets of nondepository institutions grew at only 6.7 percent.

The data clearly demonstrate the important role that depository institutions play in the credit networks of the economy. In light of this role, owners, investors, depositors, and regulators share particular concerns regarding the soundness and profitability of these institutions. The effects that solvency regulations may have on the functioning of depository intermediaries are therefore critical. If solvency regulations enhance the solidity of these institutions without adversely affecting the supply of credit, then such constraints may indeed be required. However, if these regulations reduce profitability and soundness of these institutions to the extent that the supply of credit is restricted, then the current set of solvency regulations should be relaxed or replaced with new instruments of regulation.

In the following sections, the major solvency standards for each type of depository intermediary are characterized. The aim is not to provide a complete

Table 2-3

Financial Assets of Financial Institutions (1960-1975)

| | Financial Assets ($ Billions) | | | | Annual Growth (%) |
	1960	1965	1970	1975	1960-1975
Depository Institutions					
Commercial banks	225	336	491	822	9.0
S&Ls	71	130	176	339	11.0
Mutual savings banks	41	59	79	121	7.5
Credit unions	6	11	18	37	12.9
Total	343	536	764	1319	9.4
Nondepository Institutions					
Finance companies	28	45	65	98	8.7
Security brokers and dealers	7	10	16	17	6.1
Life insurance companies	116	154	201	280	6.1
Fire and casualty insurance companies	26	37	51	77	7.5
Mutual funds	17	35	48	42	6.2
Nonsured pension funds	58	108	171	255	10.4
Total	252	389	552	769	6.7
Total, all categories	595	925	1316	2088	8.7

Source: Board of Governors of the Federal Reserve System, Flow-of-Funds Accounts 1946-1975 (1976), pp. 113-130.

list of all federal and state regulations but to illustrate their significant dimensions.[1]

This discussion will begin with asset restrictions. Asset restrictions, or portfolio constraints, aim at ensuring deposit safety. The principal focus of these constraints is asset quality and liquidity, which if controlled are thought to minimize the risk to which an institution can be exposed. Restrictions on assets and portfolios are both qualitative and quantitative in nature and can generally be characterized as either diversification, quality, or exclusion constraints. Typically, these restrictions limit the portion of funds from deposits and capital that may be employed in specific assets.

A discussion of Regulation Q restrictions and capital requirements follows. These two regulations operate in conflicting directions. Regulation Q restrictions limit the price that depository intermediaries may pay for deposits. In effect, this restriction provides a form of monopoly profits by allowing the opportunity to issue a financial liability (that is, deposits) at a rate lower than the competitive market rate. Capital requirements, on the other hand, restrict or limit the degree of leverage and thereby reduce the potential of these institutions.

Finally, the existing tax structure imposed on each institution is discussed briefly.[2] It is included here because different tax structures influence the preferred composition of the portfolio. In addition, the tax structure provides unique earnings advantages for some depository intermediaries.

Commercial Banks

Commercial banks are permitted to offer the widest mix of deposits (demand, savings, and time) and hold the widest variety of assets of all financial institutions. These institutions may be regulated by at least one of three federal agencies: the Federal Reserve Board (FRB), the Federal Deposit Insurance Corporation (FDIC), or the Comptroller of the Currency (CC), and perhaps one of 50 state agencies. For example, a commercial bank might be chartered by a state agency and examined by the FDIC.[3]

Member banks of the Federal Reserve System fall under the supervision of the Federal Reserve Board. All national banks must be members, and state-chartered banks may choose to join the system. All national and state-chartered member banks must be insured by the FDIC and are examined by either CC or FRB examiners on a regular basis.

The vast majority of commercial banks are insured by the FDIC; the current annual premium for deposit insurance is less than a percentage point of deposits. The FDIC has supervisory authority over insured state-chartered nonmember banks and is charged with examining their activities.

The CC charters and supervises national banks. Because national banks are under the jurisdiction of a federal agency, these institutions are exempt from state supervision. However, state branching restrictions do apply to national banks.

Asset Restrictions

Reserve Requirements. With some exceptions, all commercial banks are required to hold some sterile reserves or nonearning assets.[4] In general, vault cash, cash held at a Federal Reserve Bank, demand balances at other banks, and in certain instances, federal and state government obligations and long-term certificates of deposit (CDs) may be counted as reserves. Because commercial banks, in large part, determine the money supply, a primary purpose of reserve requirements is to facilitate some control of its quantity. However, reserve requirements are also designed to provide these institutions with liquid assets to support large unexpected withdrawals or buffer against loan defaults.

All members of the Federal Reserve Bank System are required to hold some reserves with the Federal Reserve Bank in their district. The actual quantity of these reserves is determined by the size and location of the bank and the mix of its deposits. Member banks must hold a larger proportion of demand deposits in reserves than time deposits. The present legal requirement for demand deposits (as of April 1979) for reserve city banks may range from a minimum of 10 percent to a maximum of 22 percent of demand deposits; for reserve country banks, the requirement may range from 7 percent to a maximum of only 14 percent. The legal reserve requirements for savings and time deposits may range presently from a minimum of 3 percent to a maximum of 10 percent.

Reserve requirements imposed on nonmember state banks vary widely from state to state. For example, nonmember Florida state banks must hold 20 percent of demand and time deposits in reserves. However, 100 percent of these reserves may be invested in U.S. securities. In contrast, nonmember North Dakota state banks must hold 8 percent of their demand deposits and 2 percent of time deposits in either vault cash or demand balances in other banks. Presently Illinois nonmember banks are not required to hold any reserves.[5]

Investment Securities Restrictions. Commercial banks may purchase and hold an unlimited quantity of federal, state, and local securities. However, some restrictions are placed on the purchase of corporate investment securities.[6] Specifically, commercial banks may not invest more than 10 percent of their capital in a set of securities issued by a single entity. This proportion may be reduced to 5 percent for certain types of securities. For the most part, banks cannot purchase or hold equity other than subsidiary equity. Investment in foreign securities is also severely restricted.

Loan Restrictions. Commercial banks may offer a full menu of business and personal loans (secured and unsecured), as well as mortgage loans. However, the loan obligations of a single entity may not be greater than 10 percent of a bank's capital.[7] A credit line may exceed 10 percent of capital as long as the amount actually advanced at any one time does not violate the 10-percent constraint. Federal funds loaned are not subject to this rule.

There are a number of exceptions to the 10-percent rule for national banks and state-regulated banks. For example, the obligations of a single borrower may range from 25 percent to 50 percent of bank capital for certain types of loans. However, these loans are unique and typically do not represent a large category within the loan portfolio. Such exceptions therefore do not provide banks with the opportunity to circumvent completely the current set of loan restrictions.

Both federal and state regulations generally limit the total quantity of funds a bank may place in real estate loans.[8] For example, national banks are currently prevented from investing more than 100 percent of their invested capital or 70 percent of their time and savings deposits (whatever is greater) into their mortgage and real estate-related loan portfolio. In addition, individual mortgage loans are constrained to not exceed 50 percent of the appraised value of the building or property (that is, the maximum loan-to-value ratio is constrained to 0.5) if the maturity of the loan is less than or equal to five years. These conditions change as the maturity of the real estate loan is extended.

Miscellaneous Asset Restrictions. Presently there are regulations that apply to personal loans and stock margin loans. Specifically, existing regulation limits both the size of personal loan commercial banks may extend to an individual and the interest rate charged. Restrictions on margin loans limit the total amount of credit extended and are expressed in terms of some percent of the market value of the underlying security. The current margin limit for stocks and convertible bonds is 50 percent.

Commercial banks are prohibited from short selling any securities. While this regulation is not particularly onerous given the current set of asset restrictions, it may become so should other portfolio restrictions be eliminated.[9] (Note that banks, in a sense, can presently short sell some securities of high quality under a repurchase agreement with a Federal Reserve Bank.)

Regulation Q Restrictions

The Federal Reserve Board's Regulation Q establishes the maximum rates of interest that all commercial banks may pay on demand deposits, savings deposits, and time deposits.[10] Currently Regulation Q constrains a commercial bank to paying an interest rate on time and savings accounts that is generally below that permitted to S&Ls, mutual savings banks, and credit unions. As of April 1979, the interest-rate ceiling on savings deposits held by commercial banks was 5 percent. Interest payments on demand deposits of commercial banks are strictly prohibited; however, banks do make implicit payments on these deposits in the form of gifts or services. For example, free checking-account services are an implicit interest payment on demand deposits. Similarly, extensive branching is (where permitted) a mechanism by which banks may circumvent, to a certain extent, this restriction by providing a more convenient location for customers.

The maximum rate permitted on time deposits varies with the size and maturity period. For time deposits of less than $100,000, the following interest ceilings were in effect as of April 1979:

Maturity	Maximum Percent
Thirty days or more, but less than ninety days	5.0
Ninety days or more, but less than one year	5.5
One year or more, but less than thirty months	6.0
Thirty months or more, but less than forty-eight months	6.5

In addition, banks may pay up to 7.5 percent and 7.75 percent on any time deposit of $1,000 or more with a maturity of up to seventy-two months and ninety-six months or more, respectively.[11] There is no interest-rate ceiling on CDs of $100,000 or more.

Although commercial banks are not permitted to pay interest on demand deposits, some commercial banks, particularly in the Northeast, have been permitted to pay interest (currently 5 percent) on a unique form of demand deposit called a "NOW account" (negotiable order of withdrawal). Mutual savings banks in the Northeast designed this form of account to attract funds. In order for commercial banks operating in that area to compete effectively for funds with mutual savings banks, these institutions were permitted to pay interest on identical accounts. Although in theory NOW accounts differ from the standard demand deposits, for the consumer these accounts have identical properties to demand deposits with the important exception of payment of interest on deposit balances. This obviously explains the sharp increase in the quantity of these accounts held by depository intermediaries located in the Northeast.

Capital Adequacy Requirements

Currently there are no regulations that establish the minimum amount of capital a bank must hold relative to its total assets. However, regulatory agencies do have statutory authority to determine "start-up" capital and surplus requirements for anyone desiring a charter to operate in the banking system.

These start-up minimum capital requirements are not set specifically as a function of some "capital to potential asset" ratio but rather are determined by the population size in which a commercial bank wants to operate. For example, in a city or town with a population exceeding 50,000 inhabitants, the minimum capital requirements generally set by the FRB and the CC is $200,000. This requirement does not specify nor limit the potential total size of the bank given the amount of capital invested. In addition, in order for a bank to gain a national charter, it must have a paid-in surplus equal to 20 percent of the value of its common and preferred stock. State-chartered banks are subject to similar regulations, but capital requirements vary widely. For example, restrictions placed on the paid-in surplus account range from 0 to 100 percent of the par value of the common stock.

Once a commercial bank commences business, regulatory agencies then use certain rule-of-thumb standards to measure the adequacy of capital (for example, capital must not fall below 5 percent of total assets). Presumably, the amount of capital funds a bank is required to hold is related to the risk it assumes; thus the magnitude of these capital adequacy standards are determined by the riskiness of the bank's portfolio and the volatility of its liabilities. For example, the FRB uses a set of capital ratio standards to analyze capital adequacy. These ratios, which specify varying amounts of capital for ten different categories of assets, range from 15 percent for short-term government securities to 100 percent for fixed assets. Each ratio is presumably determined by the perceived credit risk, market risk, and liquidity of each class of assets.[12]

Because of their organization, commercial banks may raise new capital by issuing either additional common or preferred stock or long-term debentures. In addition, member banks may borrow funds on a short-term basis from the FRB in time of need.

Tax Structure

Commercial banks are taxed as corporations by the federal government. The corporate tax rate is applied to the bank's net taxable income, which is defined as income from operating transactions (such as interest on loans and securities) and service revenue less allowable operating expenses. This figure is adjusted to make allowances for net loan losses and realized and unrealized capital gains.

A large tax benefit is realized by commercial banks holding municipal securities. Interest payments from state and local government securities are tax exempt. However, for those banks subject to a marginal federal tax rate of only 22 percent, municipals do not offer an adequate rate of return.

Commercial banks may also reduce their tax liabilities by transferring funds to bad-debt reserves to allow for expected future losses on loans. Such transfers to bad-debt reserves are treated as operating expenses and thus serve to reduce the income subject to taxes.[13]

Mutual Savings Banks

Mutual savings banks are not unlike both commercial banks and S&Ls. These depository institutions are found in many states, but the majority are located in the Northeast. Mutual banks have traditionally been regarded as depository institutions designed to promote savings.

For the most part, mutual banks are permitted to offer only time and savings accounts; however, in certain areas mutuals may also offer NOW accounts and demand deposits. Because these firms are mutually organized, depositors of mutual savings banks are owners of these institutions. Consequently, depositors share in the surplus income and capital of these firms net of any required additions to the reserve and surplus accounts. Interestingly, depositors cannot claim 100 percent of the profits earned by their deposits when they withdraw them from a mutual bank. The undistributed surplus remains with the bank in the form of permanent reserves or capital.

Until recently mutual savings banks were chartered by state agencies only.[14] Currently, there are 18 states (including Puerto Rico) that issue a mutual savings bank charter. Although all mutual savings banks are state chartered, a majority of these institutions are insured by the FDIC. The remaining mutual banks are insured by either the Federal Home Loan Bank Board (FHLBB) or by state insurance agencies. Interestingly, all mutual savings banks may join the Federal Reserve System, but at this time none have done so. Consequently, a majority of these institutions are subject to the scrutiny of the FDIC and must satisfy all FDIC requirements. However, the state regulatory agencies have primary authority over mutual savings banks.

Asset Restrictions

Reserve Requirements. The majority of state regulatory agencies require that mutual savings banks must hold some liquid assets in reserve against deposits; but the actual quantities required vary broadly from state to state. For example, Wisconsin requires that mutual savings banks hold 5 percent of their total deposit obligations in the form of liquid reserves. However, these institutions must hold at least 2.5 percent of total deposits in either cash or demand balances placed in reserve banks (that is, sterile reserves). In contrast, mutual banks chartered in Vermont must hold 3 percent of savings deposits in reserve assets; however, only two fifths of these reserves must be held in vault cash or in balances payable on demand. The remainder may be held in highly liquid interest-bearing securities. Normally, state regulatory authorities do not require mutual savings banks to hold large quantities of sterile reserves (that is, nonearning assets), yet those interest-earning assets that may be counted as reserves must be approved by the state authorities.

Investment Securities Restrictions. In most states mutual savings banks can purchase most forms of marketable debt instruments as well as common and preferred stock. State agencies normally list the types of securities eligible for purchase and the minimum standards of quality. In several states the "prudent-man" rule is applied to savings banks by the state regulatory agencies. Typically, the 10-percent diversification rule as applied to commercial banks is similarly applied to mutual savings banks.

Loan Restrictions. Mutual savings banks can make mortgage loans but are generally prohibited from making most other forms of consumer loans with the exception of loans secured by the deposits in savings banks. Strictly speaking, mutual savings banks cannot issue commercial loans.

Regulation Q Restrictions

The maximum rates that mutual savings banks may pay for most categories of deposits are set by an interagency group composed of the FRB, FDIC, and FHLBB. For the most part, mutual savings accounts are permitted by law to pay interest that is one quarter of one percent higher than similar accounts at commercial banks.[15] (See Regulation Q Restrictions of Commercial Banks.) However, for those mutual savings banks that may issue NOW accounts, the rate ceiling on these liabilities is identical to the ceiling imposed on commercial banks (5 percent). NOW accounts were "invented" by mutual savings banks and have provided an avenue by which they have overcome, to a certain extent, the relative inflexibility they face relative to other institutions in attracting funds. Indeed, prior to the change in regulation that permitted commercial banks to issue similar deposit liabilities, NOW accounts provided a considerable advantage to mutual savings banks.

Capital Adequacy Requirements

Before operations, mutual savings banks must satisfy minimum start-up capital surplus requirements. These start-up requirements are similar to those imposed on commercial banks and S&Ls by the examining authorities. While in operation, savings banks must also satisfy any capitalization standards imposed by either state regulatory agencies or the FDIC. Since all savings banks are mutually owned, they are unable to issue common stock and are often limited in their ability to issue long-term debt. Moreover, even though mutual savings banks may issue some long-term debt instruments, regulatory authorities often do not consider these funds as part of the capital base. These regulations appear to have limited the growth of these institutions. [As indicated in table 2-3, the annual growth rate of mutual savings (7.5 percent) is the lowest of all the depository intermediaries.]

Tax Structure

Mutual savings banks have been subject to the federal corporate tax since 1952. In general, the calculation of net taxable income is similar to that of commercial banks. However, savings banks, because of several unique tax shelters such as additions to reserves, have been able to reduce their effective income-tax rate. Over the last decade insured mutual savings banks have paid a lower effective tax rate than either commercial banks or S&Ls.[16]

Savings and Loan Institutions

Savings and loan institutions can be organized under two different structures: the corporate form and the mutually owned form that has no stockholders. All federally chartered S&Ls must be organized as mutuals; however, the authorities have permitted some S&Ls to convert to a corporate structure. State-chartered S&Ls can organize under either structure, but conversion from one form to another is not readily permitted. Savings and loan institutions are permitted to offer savings and time deposits, and in certain areas they may also issue NOW accounts.

As opposed to the regulatory structure of commercial banks or mutual savings banks, which are regulated under both state and federal agencies, S&Ls

are for the most part centrally regulated by the FHLBB. Member associations of the FHLBB hold approximately 98 percent of the assets of the industry. Although there are state regulations and state regulatory authorities, the number of S&Ls that are so regulated is negligible. Savings and loan institutions are also regulated to a certain extent by the Federal Savings and Loan Insurance Corporation (FSLIC), a subsidiary of the FHLBB. This agency insures the time and savings accounts of all federal and most state associations. Consequently, nearly all activities of an S&L fall under the supervision of a single federal agency. This is in contrast to the regulatory structure imposed on commercial banks where as much as three federal agencies may regulate particular activities of a single commercial bank.

Asset Restrictions

Reserve Requirements. Federal Home Loan Bank Board-member S&Ls are required to hold liquid reserves against their deposit accounts. These reserves are designed to further institutional liquidity and ensure a steady supply of money to mortgages. Currently for member S&Ls, approximately 6.0 percent of total savings accounts must be placed in some form of liquid reserve. This liquid reserve may include vault cash, deposits held at commercial banks, and interest-earning government securities. However, the amount of reserves that must be held in cash or highly liquid, short-term, interest-earning assets is approximately 2.5 percent of the deposit base.

Under current regulation, the liquidity reserve may range from a minimum of 4 percent to a maximum of 10 percent of withdrawable deposit obligations. Even though a majority of these reserves can be held in interest-earning assets, the FHLBB must first approve the obligations.

Because a large majority of state- and federal-chartered S&Ls belong to the FHLBB system, liquidity requirements are uniform across these institutions. That is, all federal-chartered and state-chartered FSLIC-insured S&Ls are subject to identical liquidity requirements. This is in sharp contrast to FDIC-insured commercial banks where reserve requirements may widely vary by sta ; and charter.

State-chartered associations that are not members of the FHLBB system are governed by state law and are not subject to the FHLBB liquidity requirements. Presently there are only 16 states that require nonmember S&Ls to hold some reserves against deposit accounts.

Investment Securities Restrictions. Investment opportunities for S&Ls are severely limited. Nearly all associations are prohibited from buying corporate bonds. The investment securities that are eligible for purchase are restricted to high quality and are generally limited to short maturity. Savings and loan associations may purchase any quantity of federal, state, and local securities as long as the aggregate quantity does not exceed 20 percent of assets; they cannot purchase or hold equity.

Loan Restrictions. Savings and loan associations were originally organized as mutual building associations. This historical tradition is a significant factor in the determination of the portfolio composition of these institutions and their present portfolio requirements. Current loan restrictions basically promote the investment in small local residential areas. In fact, federally chartered S&Ls must make the majority of their funds available for residential real estate loans. Specifically, a federally chartered S&L must invest 80 percent of its assets in mortgages or otherwise be penalized.

In making real estate loans, S&Ls are restricted to a 100-mile radius of their principal office or the boundaries of the state it operates in, whatever is greater. Within the real estate-related loan categories, a loan-diversification rule is imposed. For instance, until recently loans of 90 percent or more of the appraised value of a one-to-four-unit house could not exceed $55,000, nor could the aggregate amount of these loans exceed 30 percent of total assets.

Savings and loan associations may provide loans to both builders and individuals for one-family homes. However, the maturity of these loans to builders and individuals is three and five years, respectively. The aggregate quantity of both loan categories cannot exceed 20 percent of total assets. Savings and loans may also finance mobile homes and offer secured personal loans of short maturity; however, the aggregate amount of these loans is limited due to mortgage requirements discussed earlier.

State regulations on loans are similar to federal law; however, a few states do permit S&Ls to invest in some form of personal unsecured, any-purpose loan. These loans, however, are generally subject to a maximum term of five years and a maximum size of $5,000. In the aggregate, these loans cannot be greater than 8 to 10 percent of the total assets of the S&Ls.

Regulation Q Restrictions

The FHLBB in conjunction with an interagency board establishes maximum interest rates S&Ls may pay on time and savings accounts. As of April 1979 these maximum limits were 5.25 percent for regular savings accounts, 5.75 percent for three- to twelve-month time deposit accounts, 6.50 percent for time deposits of twelve months up to thirty months with a $1,000 minimum, and 6.75 percent for time deposits of greater than thirty months up to forty-eight months with a $1,000 minimum. For CDs of less than $100,000 maturing between forty-nine months and seventy-two months, and seventy-three months up to ninety-six months, S&Ls are restricted to paying a maximum of 7.5 percent and 7.75 percent, respectively. Savings and loan associations may pay up to 8.0 percent on deposits of ninety-six months or more. Interest rates on CDs of $100,000 or more are not regulated; however, current regulation does limit the aggregate amount of these deposits that an S&L may issue.

Capital Adequacy Requirements

Before a federally chartered S&L may begin operations, it must satisfy minimum capital (or reserve) requirements established by the FHLBB. Similar capital requirements are imposed on state-chartered S&Ls by either the FHLBB or the state counterpart. These requirements are designed to ensure the solvency of these institutions. Savings and loan associations must also satisfy capital adequacy requirements during their years of operations. These requirements are a function of the size and age of the institution; however, after a period of time all member S&Ls must maintain a capital reserve of at least 5.5 percent of assets.

The initial source of capital for a mutual association is typically the organizers of the firm. However, regulators do place limits on how rapidly the organizers may withdraw their "capital" during the first few years of business. While in operation, the primary source of capital for mutual associations is retained earnings (*note:* some can sell long-term debt); stock associations, however, may also raise external long-term capital by issuing additional debt or stock. All member S&Ls may borrow from the FHLBB up to 25 percent of their total withdrawable funds at rates that fluctuate with the rates prevailing in the capital markets for similar obligations.

Tax Structure

Savings and loan associations were made subject to the federal tax laws in the same year as mutual savings banks. Net taxable income is calculated in a similar fashion. In general, the effective tax rate of S&Ls has increased over the last ten years. This increase can be attributed to the elimination of tax provisions that permitted large transfers to bad-debt reserves. These changes in the tax provisions resulted in significant increases in the taxes paid by all thrift institutions, namely, S&Ls and mutual savings banks. Currently, available tax shelters are generally the same for thrift institutions and commercial banks. This places S&Ls at a considerable disadvantage given the restrictions placed on the use of their funds (for example, the 80-percent mortgage rule).

Credit Unions

Credit unions are cooperative organizations chartered by either the federal government [National Credit Union Administration (NCUA)] or a state agency.[17] These institutions are formed by individuals with a common bond to meet their need for credit financed through members' savings. Credit unions are supervised on a two-tiered level, as are other depository institutions. Nationally, the NCUA is responsible for chartering, supervising, and insuring credit unions. The NCUA thus has examination responsibilities and regulatory powers similar to the other regulatory agencies at the federal level. All 50 states charter credit unions; typically, the state bank-regulatory agencies supervise them.

All credit unions issue share accounts, and a number of state-chartered credit unions are permitted to issue time deposits. In some isolated cases, credit unions can issue share draft accounts on which members can write third-party-payment instruments while receiving interest on the balance. This deposit liability is analogous to a nationwide NOW account. Generally, credit union share certificates and share accounts are paid rates of interest (dividends) well above those paid on conventional accounts. These powers give credit unions a full set of deposit accounts and certificates that have not been available to other depository institutions.

Asset Restrictions

Reserve Requirements. Federally chartered credit unions are not required to hold liquid reserves against their share accounts; however, they must hold cash reserves to support their share draft accounts. (Share draft accounts are not widespread so credit unions hold no sterile reserves.) This generally holds true for state-chartered credit unions as well. Because their assets are, for the most part, short term in nature, such restrictions are not viewed as needed to ensure the solvency of the credit union. Nonetheless, because there is concern for liquidity in general, state credit union leagues have been organized and have formed the Credit Union National Association. The principal function of the state and national credit union leagues is to aid in matching the needs of credit unions long on deposits with those in need of loanable funds. These leagues may also provide investment advice and in some cases provide operational support.

Investment Securities Restrictions. Credit unions are restricted from investing in any form of corporate securities. They are permitted, however, to hold government treasury issues of short maturity.

Loan Restrictions. The principal form of investment for credit unions has traditionally been the installment loan. Installment loans are short term in nature and are amortized monthly. Accordingly, this type of loan reduces a credit union's need for liquid reserves. Most state-chartered credit unions now have the authority to offer first mortgages on one-to-four-family residential dwellings for up to thirty years. Although this is a serious challenge to the liquidity of many credit unions, mortgages will offer more diversification in their loan portfolio. In general, federal credit unions may issue unsecured loans with maturities of up to five years and secured loans with maturities of up to ten years. Credit unions are required to fix the maximum amount that may be loaned to any one member, but the maximum may not exceed 10 percent of the credit union's total capital. This rule is similar to the 10-percent diversification rule imposed on banks and S&Ls.

Regulation Q Restrictions

Federal credit unions are permitted to pay a maximum rate of 7-percent dividends on member share accounts. The dividend ceiling imposed on state-chartered credit unions ranges from 4 percent to no limit. Although not all credit unions pay the highest rate, approximately half pay between 6 and 7 percent. The interest rates that state-chartered credit unions may pay on time deposits is generally higher than the rates permitted on share accounts and are significantly higher than the rate ceilings imposed on other institutions. This favorable rate differential for credit unions not only appeals to current and potential members but also allows credit unions to retain and attract funds when other institutions are suffering from disintermediation.

Capital Adequacy Requirements

Prior to operations, the NCUA is charged with establishing the business potential of a new federal association and therefore the amount of shares that must be pledged to the institution. In theory, these shares are analogous to a corporation's equity capital because there can be no guarantee of dividends or repayment of principal. In practice, however, these shares resemble time and savings deposits that yield fixed interest payments.

Once a credit union begins operations, it is required to satisfy certain capital (surplus) adequacy standards. For example, federal credit unions are required to set aside a proportion of net earnings (before dividends) as reserves until these reserves accumulate to 6.0 percent of their risk assets. This reserve is designed to protect the members' shares. (*Note:* A credit union's reserve fund includes loss reserves, supplemental reserves, and undistributed profits.) For the most part, all federal and state credit unions are permitted to borrow from other credit unions or from other sources an amount up to 50 percent of capital and surplus.

Tax Structure

Credit unions are generally tax exempt. The income and financial assets of a federal credit union may not be taxed by any level of government; however, some state-chartered credit unions may be taxed. In those states that do tax state-chartered credit unions, the tax rate is normally the same rate that is applied to thrift institutions. It is important to note that because credit unions generally do not pay taxes, municipal bonds would not be an attractive asset for their portfolios, even if permitted.

Summary

Commercial banks are required to hold a nonnegligible percentage of their assets in the form of nonearning reserves. In contrast, thrift institutions typically do not face such severe reserve requirements. On the other hand, commercial banks have a broader choice among maturity, credit risk, and type of asset they can acquire, while thrift associations in general are forced by environment and regulation to emphasize long-term consumer loans, principally mortgages. Commercial banks have the option of raising capital externally whereas the capital or reserve position of mutual thrift associations tends to be a passive residual of net income that the associations are able to retain. The capital positions of both commercial banks and thrift institutions are regularly reviewed by the authorities.

Both commercial banks and thrift institutions issue deposits that are subject to interest-rate ceilings. These ceilings differ generally by 0.25 percent.

Member banks have access to the Federal Reserve for obtaining emergency funds, while S&Ls can obtain funds from the FHLBB. Savings and loan associations have the privilege of borrowing up to 25 percent of their total withdrawable deposits from their regional Home Loan bank. Such advances are available at various maturities and at rates set by the board. In general, mutual savings banks do not have the opportunity to borrow from either the FRB or the FHLBB (except for a few banks that have joined the FHLBB system). Credit unions, on the other hand, have the opportunity to raise liquid assets through the Credit Union National Association. (Recall that these liquid assets are generated from the formation of state credit union leagues or a central liquidity facility.)

Federal income taxes as a percent of net income have generally been rising for insured S&Ls. Commercial banks pay slightly less income tax, and mutual savings banks even less. Credit unions pay no income tax at the federal level (see figure 2-1).

In this overview of depository intermediaries and existing solvency standards, we have ignored the market conditions and structure of the industry. For example, we made no mention of the competitive environment nor the volatility of deposit liabilities that in part influence the portfolio behavior of an institution. However, these factors impinge on all institutions in a similar way. As such, a comparative analysis can ignore these considerations. The focus of this study is to investigate the impact of solvency regulations on the investment opportunity set and the profitability of each type of depository intermediary. By abstracting the investigation from the competitive conditions of the market-

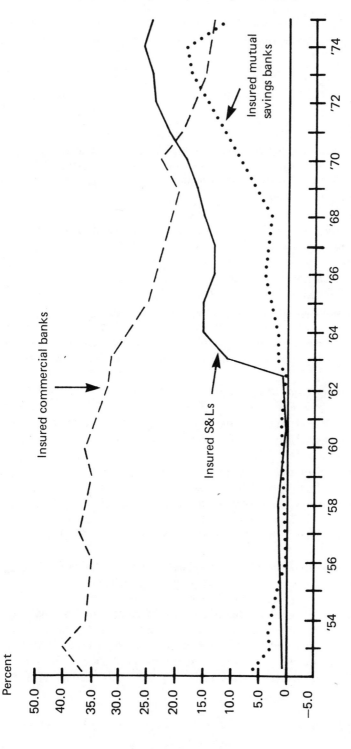

Percent

Figure 2-1. Federal Income Taxes as a Percent of Net Income.

Source: M.E. Bedford, "Federal Taxation of Financial Institutions," *Monthly Review*, Federal Reserve Bank of Kansas City (June 1976), p. 5. Reprinted with permission.

place, the analysis can more clearly examine the effect that regulations have on each institution and more readily contrast these effects across each type of depository institution.

Notes

1. See J. Vitarello, "The Regulatory and Legal Structure," in *Evaluation of the Social Impact of Regulation,* pp. 258-363, for an exhaustive survey of the entire structure of regulations pertaining to depository intermediaries. See also G.H. Hempel and J.B. Yawitz, *Financial Management of Financial Institutions* (Englewood Cliffs, N.J.: Prentice-Hall, 1977), pp. 69-152.

2. For a more complete discussion on the federal tax structure imposed on depository intermediaries, see M.E. Bedford, "Federal Taxation of Financial Institutions," *Monthly Review,* Federal Reserve Bank of Kansas City (June 1976), pp. 3-15.

3. For a discussion on the regulatory structure imposed on commercial banks, see E.W. Reed et al., *Commercial Banking,* pp. 25-30.

4. For a comparative analysis of reserve requirements imposed on each type of depository intermediary, see L.S. Mayne, "The Deposit Reserve Requirement Recommendations of the Commission on Financial Structure and Regulation: An Analysis and Critique," *Journal of Bank Research* 4 (1973):41-51.

5. The reserve requirements on deposits of member banks are published monthly in the *Federal Reserve Bulletin* (Washington, D.C.: Board of Governors of the Federal Reserve System). For a review of reserve requirements for nonmember commercial banks, see C.J. Prestopino, *The Impact of Differential Reserve Requirements,* pp. 42-47.

6. An *investment security* is defined generally as a debt obligation of an established corporation. Speculative securities, as defined by the bond rating companies, are normally excluded from purchase. See E.J. Roddy, "Legal and Regulatory Constraints upon Employment of Bank Funds," in *The Bankers' Handbook,* eds. W.H. Baughn and C.E. Walker (Homewood, Ill.: Dow-Jones-Irwin, 1966), pp. 549-560.

7. The total capital of a commercial bank, which serves as the lending base, is defined as the sum of the equity account, surplus fund, capital notes, and debentures. Capital notes and debentures must be subordinated to all deposit liabilities. The surplus fund is the sum of paid-in surplus, undivided profits, loan-loss reserves, evaluation reserves for securities, and the reserves for contingencies. Note that a mutual association such as a mutual savings bank or S&L does not have an equity account. Therefore the surplus account or surplus fund (and long-term debt in some cases) represents the capital of these institutions.

8. A *real estate loan* is defined as any loan in which real property represents the primary security for the loan. This definition is used throughout this chapter.

9. The restrictions on margin loans, as well as the prohibition of short selling, also apply to all other depository intermediaries. These restrictions will not, therefore, be mentioned in the subsequent discussion.

10. Regulation Q rate ceilings are published monthly in the *Federal Reserve Bulletin.*

11. In late 1978 Congress permitted commercial banks to issue six-month, variable-rate savings certificates that yield the T-bill rate that prevailed one week prior to issue.

12. See E.W. Reed et al., *Commercial Banking,* pp. 402-409, for a discussion of the FRB's capital adequacy test.

13. Until recently the tax laws permitted banks to calculate additions to the loan-loss reserve in a fashion that was not necessarily related to expected future losses. Banks could thus reduce the effective tax on net income by transferring a substantial amount of income to the loss reserve. This law has recently been changed so that banks no longer have this advantage. See M.E. Bedford, "Federal Taxation of Financial Institutions," pp. 3-15, for an analysis of the recent changes in the tax code dealing with the loss reserve.

14. The 1978 Financial Institutions Act passed recently by Congress provides for a national charter of mutual savings banks.

15. Mutual savings banks and S&Ls may pay a one half of one percent higher rate on time deposits with maturities ranging from twelve months to thirty months with a minimum deposit of $1,000. In addition both thrift institutions may generally pay one quarter of one percent higher rate on the recently introduced six-month variable-rate savings certificates (see note 11).

16. See M.E. Bedford, "Federal Taxation of Financial Institutions," pp. 3-15.

17. See M.J. Flannery, *An Economic Evaluation of Credit Unions in the United States* (Boston: Federal Reserve Bank of Boston Research Report No. 54, 1974), for an extensive discussion and analysis of the institutional environment and behavior of credit unions. This section relies primarily on his work.

3 Effects of Solvency Regulation on a Depository Intermediary

In this chapter we analyze how solvency regulations affect the investment opportunities and risk-return characteristics of a depository intermediary. To conduct this analysis, we will construct a simple risk-return model of an intermediary. This model permits an examination of the effects that solvency regulations have on both portfolio risk and the total risk of the intermediary.

Portfolio risk of an intermediary, that is, the profit risk assumed by invested capital of the firm, depends primarily on the composition of the asset portfolio, how returns vary, and the amount of available capital relative to deposits. The primary components of portfolio risk are: (1) interest-rate risk, which is determined by the maturity structure of the portfolio; (2) default and market risk, which is a function of the type of assets held by the firm; and (3) cost-of-funds risk, the uncertainty associated with the average and marginal cost of deposit liabilities. This component of portfolio risk is determined primarily by the structure of interest rates prevailing in the capital markets and the level of deposit-rate ceilings imposed on an intermediary by regulation.[1]

Likewise, the total risk of an intermediary, that is, the risk of insolvency, depends largely on the firm's selection of assets, the quantity and price of liabilities, and the amount of capital the firm has available to offset any potential losses. Generally speaking, the risk of insolvency is defined by the probability of losses of capital that may occur as a result of the firm's choosing a particular portfolio/leverage combination.

As suggested earlier, an immediate goal of solvency regulation is to reduce both the portfolio risk and total risk of the firm. Consequently, the major solvency instruments aim at controlling or influencing those key factors that determine these risks.

The analysis proceeds in the following steps. First, we discuss briefly the assumptions used in the analysis. Second, a risk-return portfolio model is used to investigate the effects of asset restrictions on the investment opportunity frontier of an intermediary. Third, Regulation Q ceilings and leverage constraints are introduced, and the risk-return characteristics of a depository intermediary are then derived. These characteristics can be summarized in the efficient risk-return locus of the firm. To derive properly the risk-return locus of an intermediary, all solvency regulations must be incorporated in a model. Accordingly, asset restrictions, deposit-rate ceilings, and leverage constraints are treated simultaneously. Fourth, the risk-return locus is compared to the locus of an intermediary (say, a mutual fund) operating in an unconstrained environment.

Based on this comparison, the issue of whether a constrained intermediary can compete successfully with the unconstrained sector for new capital is addressed. Finally, the results are summarized at the end of the chapter. Chapters 4 and 5 then present empirical findings of the effects of solvency regulations on the risk-return characteristics of each type of depository intermediary.

To provide perspective on the analysis that follows, it is important to emphasize that the primary concern of this study is not the reaction of the firm to a regulatory change.[2] (We present such an analysis briefly in appendix A.) Rather, this study is concerned principally with the quantitative and qualitative effects of solvency regulations on the investment opportunities and the risk-return characteristics of depository intermediaries. Accordingly, our focus is the nature of the constrained risk-return locus of each type of intermediary relative to the unconstrained situation, and the sensitivity of these loci to changes in the regulatory standards. Our goal is therefore to examine and describe the "external" effects on the firm of solvency regulations.

The major assumptions used to construct the model and to carry out the analysis are as follows:

1. Total deposit size is assumed to be under the control of management. That is, the quantity of total deposits raised by the firm to support the purchase of financial assets is a choice variable.[3] As a first step, we will assume that the liability side of the balance sheet is fixed. Although this is somewhat extreme, it allows the analysis to isolate the impacts of asset restrictions on the investment frontier. It further permits the isolation of the risk characteristics of this frontier without giving consideration to alternative deposit levels. However, in a later section, we will treat explicitly total deposit size as a choice variable.

2. The firm behaves as a risk-averse decision maker.[4] The firm's behavior reflects the common interests of owners and managers, which in many cases are one and the same. It is further assumed that an intermediary bases its portfolio and leverage decisions on the expectation and standard deviation of end-of-period returns to invested capital (or surplus in the case of mutual institutions).[5]

3. An intermediary acts as if all risky assets were traded in competitive markets; thus each firm treats the ex-ante rates of return on each asset as given. Although this assumption may not hold in every market completely (for example, small commercial loans), it appears to be realistic as a first approximation.[6] We should mention that introducing market imperfections into the analysis does not change our results. Accordingly, we can safely ignore this complexity in the following analysis.[7]

Before proceeding, it is appropriate to discuss more fully the behavior of the firm. As we mentioned earlier, we assume the firm (whether it is a stock or a mutual intermediary) behaves as a risk-averse decision maker or expected utility maximizer with end-of-period returns to invested capital as the principal argument. We further assume that all portfolio and leverage decisions reflect the risk aversion and interests of both management and owners. The decision process of the firm will thus proceed in the following way: Management first identifies the firm's efficient risk-return opportunity locus, or the set of investment and leverage combinations that yield the highest return to invested capital per unit of risk. It will then select a particular point on this locus on the basis of its interests and the interests of the owners. Once the end-of-period return is realized, the surplus is then distributed to the stockholders or, in the case of mutual organizations, to both borrowers and depositors.

One may object to this assumption and argue that management may in fact make its portfolio/leverage decisions to maximize the market value of the firm rather than a risk-averse decision function. Therefore, the interests and risk preferences of management will not enter into the decision process. However, our assumptions concerning the decision process appear to be realistic for several reasons. First, the vast majority of commercial banks and S&Ls are small and closely held. Ownership and management is therefore one and the same. Second, these same institutions are not generally traded on an organized stock exchange. Therefore, it is not clear how their market value is determined.[8] Third, in the case of mutual organizations, management and ownership is clearly separate. Once the firm is established, depositors/owners have little or no control over management with respect to investment and leverage decisions. This of course does not imply that management may be indifferent to the interests of depositors/owners but only that management has wide latitude in its decisions.

Asset Restrictions

In this section each general type of asset or portfolio restriction is analyzed in terms of its effect on an intermediary's efficient frontier.[9] Specifically, each type of portfolio restriction is introduced into an intermediary's investment opportunity set, and the characteristics of the resulting investment frontier are described.

The first section describes the characteristics of an intermediary's efficient frontier when there are no constraints whatsoever. The characteristics of the unconstrained frontier are of course well known, but it is important to review them so that the effects of particular asset restrictions can be compared to this benchmark. Following this, the analysis then proceeds by introducing quantity constraints (for example, a 10-percent diversification rule) into the opportunity set. Reserve requirements are introduced subsequently. Finally, the effects of asset restrictions and reserve requirements are analyzed in terms of the profitability and risk of the firm.

Unconstrained Efficient Frontier

An intermediary's expected end-of-period net operating rate of return on a fixed pool of available funds is determined largely by the composition of its asset portfolio, the expected rate of return of each asset, and the expected operating costs associated with the portfolio. (We will ignore for the moment the cost of funds.) In symbols, an intermediary's expected net operating return on total available funds is

$$\bar{R}_A = \frac{\sum\limits_{i=1}^{N} C_i(1 + \bar{R}_i) - C}{C} \tag{3.1}$$

where

C = fixed pool of available funds, which includes total deposit liabilities
   D and total invested capital or surplus *K*.

C_i = amount of total available funds invested in the *i*th asset, where total
   available funds is defined as total liabilities and capital less intermediary premises, other real estate and other assets and is equal to
   cash and due from banks plus loans and investments.[10]

$\bar{R}_i$ = expected rate of return of the *i*th asset net of expected operating
   costs associated with acquiring and servicing the *i*th asset.

N = total number of assets in the portfolio.

— = expectation operator.

Let

$$X_i = \frac{C_i}{C}, \quad i = 1, 2, ..., N$$

so that

$$\sum\limits_{i=1}^{N} X_i = 1 \tag{3.2}$$

Thus X_i is the proportion of total available funds invested in the *i*th asset.

Using the definition of X_i, we can write the firm's uncertain net operating rate of return on its portfolio, $\tilde{R}_A$, given a particular allocation of funds X_i $(i = 1, 2, ..., N)$ as

$$\tilde{R}_A = \sum\limits_{i=1}^{N} X_i \tilde{R}_i \tag{3.3}$$

The expected net operating rate of return and the variance of rate of return on this portfolio are, respectively,

$$\bar{R}_A = \sum_{i=1}^{N} X_i \bar{R}_i \qquad (3.4)$$

and

$$\sigma_A^2 = \sum_{i=1}^{N} \sum_{j=1}^{N} X_i X_j \sigma_{ij} \qquad (3.5)$$

where

σ_{ij} = covariance of returns between the ith and jth assets. We will assume that the variance-covariance matrix of the joint distribution of returns is positive definite.[11]

At the beginning of each period, an intermediary will allocate its total available funds to particular assets so that its portfolio yields a $(\bar{R}_A, \sigma_A)$ combination that is a member of the efficient frontier. Before discussing the unconstrained efficient frontier, a brief mention of the net rate of return of each asset is appropriate. The expected single-period rate of return of the ith asset is defined as

$$\bar{R}_i = \frac{\bar{P}_{i1} - P_{i0}}{P_{i0}} + \frac{\bar{I}_i}{P_{i0}} - \frac{\bar{Lo}_i}{P_{i0}} - \frac{\bar{E}_i}{P_{i0}}$$

where

$\dfrac{(\bar{P}_{i1} - P_{i0})}{P_{i0}}$ = expected realized or unrealized capital gain or loss on the ith asset. The capital value of the ith asset will change due to a change in either interest rates or perception of the quality of the asset at the end of the period by either the market or intermediary. Note that the capital value of a loan will also change as the loan is amortized. The term P_{it} is the value of the ith asset (security or loan) at the beginning of the tth period.

$\bar{I}_i$ = expected interest payments received on the outstanding principal of the ith asset (or dividends received if the asset represents equity).

$\bar{Lo}_i$ = expected dollar losses from partial or total default of interest and/or principal owed.

$\overline{E}_i$ = expected operating costs of acquiring and servicing the ith asset over the period. For example, these costs may be brokerage fees or expenses required to support an investment portfolio manager or loan officer.

As the expression for rate of return indicates, all factors that contribute to the net return of a financial asset and relevant to an intermediary are incorporated. Normally, the definition of rate of return ignores operating expenses and includes realized capital gains and dividend/interest returns only. The definition used here, however, includes expected losses and operating costs of acquiring and servicing each asset. Any default of principal or deviation of realized operating costs from the expected will lead to a lower realized rate of return. (In a later section we also include the expected cost of liabilities.)

In addition, the definition of rate of return includes *both* realized and unrealized capital gains or losses. On the one hand, any decrease in capital value, whether realized or unrealized, represents an opportunity cost to an intermediary. On the other hand, any realized or unrealized increase in capital value of an asset translates into an increase in the value of the firm and a gain to its owners. In either case, potential changes in capital value expose the firm and its owners to loss of income and capital. Clearly management of the firm recognizes this risk when it evaluates, say, the required contract rate on a loan or the appropriate price of a bond.

Assuming a fixed amount of total available funds and a perfect short-selling mechanism, the intermediary's efficient investment frontier can be derived in the following manner

$$\underset{[X_i]}{\text{minimize}} \ \tfrac{1}{2} \sum_i^N \sum_j^N X_i X_j \sigma_{ij} \qquad (3.6)$$

subject to equations 3.4 and 3.2

$$\overline{R}_A = \sum_i^N X_i \overline{R}_i$$

$$1 = \sum_i^N X_i$$

where

N = the total number of risky assets in the universe of financial assets.

$\overline{R}_A$ = the prescribed expected net operating rate of return on available funds. (The entire frontier can be found by varying $\overline{R}_A$ over its feasible range.)

Thus the firm will choose an allocation of total available funds X_i^* invested in each of the N available securities and loans that minimize the risk of its portfolio for a given target return. This basic portfolio problem can be rewritten in Lagrangean form

$$\Omega = \tfrac{1}{2} \sum_i^N \sum_j^N X_i X_j \sigma_{ij} + \lambda_1 (\overline{R}_A - \sum_i^N X_i \overline{R}_i) + \lambda_2 (1 - \sum_i^N X_i) \qquad (3.7)$$

where

λ_j = Lagrangean multiplier corresponding to the jth constraint.

Differentiating equation 3.7 with respect to X_i ($i = 1, 2, ..., N$) leads to $N + 2$ linear equations in $N + 2$ unknowns. It is well known that the solutions to this set of equations represent the optimal allocations of total available funds into each asset i ($i = 1, 2, ..., N$) for a family of efficient portfolios. These allocations are linear functions of the expected net operating rate of return $\overline{R}_A$ and the variances/covariances of the joint distribution of asset returns only. Thus given any target rate of return $\overline{R}_A$, the allocation of funds is determined uniquely by parameters that are in large part beyond an intermediary's control.

The solutions to this basic portfolio problem define the efficient frontier (see figure 3-1). Therefore, the efficient frontier is a function of the target rates of return and the market-determined parameters of returns on each asset. In general, the efficient frontier represents the maximum advantages that an intermediary may gain from diversification; thus the firm cannot possibly achieve a higher expected return on its portfolio per unit of portfolio risk.

Short-selling Restrictions

The unconstrained frontier of efficient portfolios will serve as the basic benchmark by which we can compare and contrast the effects of each type of asset or portfolio restriction.

To begin, consider the restriction on short selling. This regulation, which limits an intermediary to taking only nonnegative positions in its assets, is designed to restrict speculative activity on the part of an intermediary. Presumably, permitting an intermediary to sell a financial asset short could lead to excessive risk taking and a higher total risk of the firm. However, in practice this constraint reduces the number of assets that are included in each efficient portfolio. As such, this restriction eliminates a number of opportunities for diversification and leads to larger portfolio risk for a given return. The net effect is therefore to expose an intermediary to loss of income and capital since the firm is now unable to protect, to the extent possible, its portfolio from expected changes in the value of its financial assets.

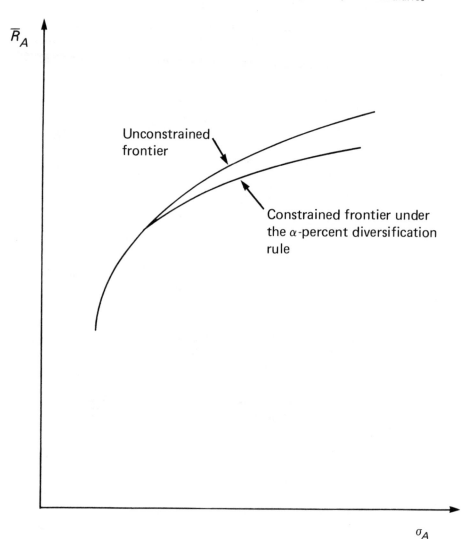

Figure 3-1. Risk-Return Efficient Frontier (Risky Assets Only)

The restrictions on short selling can be introduced into the firm's investment opportunity set by imposing the condition that all allocations must be nonnegative (that is, $X_i \geqslant 0$). The intermediary's efficient frontier can then be derived by working through the optimization problem described by equation 3.7, subject to the nonnegativity constraints.

Although the basic shape of the frontier remains under this type of constraint, it will nonetheless yield a less favorable return per unit of risk to the firm than the unconstrained frontier. Basically, this regulation has eliminated any opportunity the firm may have had to reduce the risk of its portfolio through short selling certain assets.[12] In practical terms, the restriction on short selling significantly reduces the number of assets positioned in each portfolio thereby increasing portfolio risk for any given return. Accordingly, the constrained frontier lies below the unconstrained frontier over the entire feasible range of portfolio risk; the net result is less efficient use of an intermediary's available funds and higher risk exposure.

Quantity and Exclusion Constraints

In this section we describe the basic characteristics and effects of several regulations designed largely to ensure that an intermediary's portfolio is sufficiently diversified. In theory, the basic purpose of these regulations, which generally limit the quantity of funds an intermediary may allocate to a single asset, is to reduce the amount of capital that the firm may expose to any one borrower. Presumably, this ensures that the firm will not go into bankruptcy whenever any single borrower defaults.

In practice, however, quantity restrictions may interfere with the optimal allocation of funds into each frontier portfolio. Of course, the extent to which these regulations do interfere will depend on the risk-diversifying properties of the restricted assets and the size of the constraints. Nonetheless, it is likely that the constraints do contribute unnecessarily to the total risk of the firm.

A quantity constraint may be depicted as

$$X_i = \alpha_i, \quad 0 \leqslant \alpha_i \leqslant 1 \tag{3.8}$$

for $i = 1, 2, ..., M$ restricted assets (for example, commercial loans). While the X_is in equation 3.8 are defined in terms of total available funds, diversification constraints are defined generally in terms of capital.[13] We can make the appropriate transformation in equation 3.8 by multiplying the original constraints by $1/(1 + L)$, where $L = D/K$. Thus α_i in equation 3.8 equals $[1/(1 + L)]$ α_i' where α_i' limits an intermediary to investing no more than α_i' percent of its capital in the ith asset.

An intermediary's efficient frontier subject to this form of regulation can be derived by minimizing the risk of the portfolio, equation 3.6, subject to the constraints, equations 3.2, 3.4, and 3.8. Introducing these quantity constraints into the Lagrangean, equation 3.7, yields

$$\Omega = \tfrac{1}{2} \sum_i^N \sum_j^N X_i X_j \sigma_{ij} + \lambda_1 (\overline{R}_A - \sum_i^N X_i \overline{R}_i) + \lambda_2 (1 - \sum_i^N X_i) \tag{3.9}$$

$$+ \sum_i^M \lambda_i (\alpha_i - X_i)$$

The solutions to equation 3.9, which define all legitimate efficient portfolios, represent the optimal investment proportions of each risky asset positioned in each frontier portfolio. In contrast to the unconstrained case (equation 3.7), however, the solutions are now a function of α_i, the quantity constraints imposed by regulation.

Conceivably, the quantity constraints (α_i) may not affect the optimal allocation of funds to each portfolio. However, it is more than likely that at least one inequality constraint is binding; namely, an unconstrained allocation (X_i^*) is greater than its respective constraint ($X_i^* \nleqslant \alpha_i$). Therefore, the solutions to equation 3.7 will differ, and perhaps significantly, from the solutions to equation 3.9. As such, the respective efficient frontier derived from these solutions will diverge. Indeed, as more constraints are imposed on the allocation of funds, the distance between the unconstrained and constrained frontiers will increase (see figure 3-1). At best, therefore, these regulations will have no effect on the allocation of funds and are accordingly redundant; at worst, however, these constraints will increase the risk of each portfolio and therefore the solvency risk of the firm.

Some regulations purposely exclude certain assets from the investment set of an intermediary. These regulations have the same basic effects as quantity constraints since exclusion constraints are in fact quantity constraints for $\alpha_i = 0$. Surely in this case the intermediary is worse off.

For example, assume that only three assets X, Y, and Z are available for purchase and an intermediary is restricted by regulation to investing in only two assets X and Y—the high-risk asset is excluded from the opportunity set. The constrained opportunity frontier might look like X-Y in figure 3-2. (Note the correlation between X and Y is less than 1.) If the opportunity set is now expanded and the firm is permitted to purchase asset Z in any quantity (restricting this quantity would not change the result), along with the other two assets, the frontier might look like X-Z which clearly dominates the X-Y frontier. Because of the portfolio effect, the firm is better off, and certainly no worse off, after the change in regulation. In fact, if the regulators limited the total risk of the portfolio to σ_A', the inclusion of asset Z in the investment opportunity set results in a more favorable efficient frontier.

Although it is conceivable that short-selling restrictions and quantity and exclusion constraints may eliminate some highly "risky" securities and/or loans from an intermediary's investment set, on balance these regulations do not achieve the desired result; that is, overall portfolio risk rises when these regulations are imposed. Perhaps regulators could, on a very selective basis, reduce the riskiness of the portfolio through these means; however, to do so successfully would require complete knowledge of the risk-diversifying or stablizing properties of each asset (that is, how each asset covaries with others). In light of this requirement, it appears these regulations should be eliminated.

While in theory it is quite clear that any constraints imposed on the investment opportunities set will produce undesirable effects, in practice the size or magnitude of these effects is of primary importance. For example, it may well

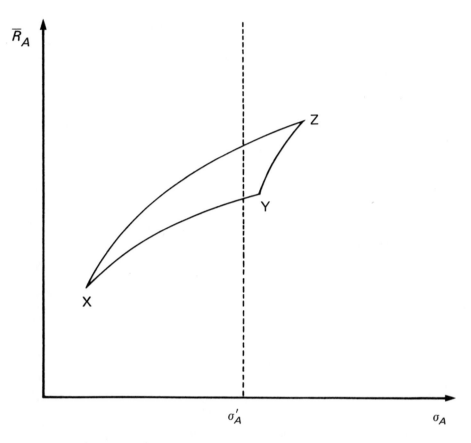

Figure 3-2. Efficient Frontier (Risky Assets Only) after Elimination of an Asset-exclusion Constraint

be the case that regulators have successfully identified those assets that contribute substantial risk to the portfolio and have eliminated them from the set of assets that are available for purchase. We will examine whether this is the case in chapter 5.

Reserve Requirements

Reserve regulations compel an intermediary to allocate a fixed portion of its total available funds to a risk-free asset. Some reserve standards specify that reserve assets must be strictly cash, whereas in other instances some portion of reserves may be allocated to a riskless security that earns a positive return. In either case, reserve requirements reduce the total quantity of funds available for investment in risky assets. The effects of these requirements on the efficient frontier are described as follows.

To begin, let β' be the proportion of total available funds that must be allocated to cash to satisfy a reserve requirement. An intermediary's expected net operating rate of return on total available funds after the imposition of a reserve requirement $\bar{R}_A$ is then

$$R'_A = \frac{\sum\limits_{i=1}^{N} C_i(1-\beta')\bar{R}_i}{C} \tag{3.10}$$

where

$\beta' = [L/(1+L)]\,\beta$

β = the weighted average reserve requirement imposed on D.
These weights depend on the relative mix of deposit liabilities.

Thus

$$\bar{R}'_A = \sum\limits_{i=1}^{N} X_i(1-\beta')\bar{R}_i \tag{3.11}$$

or

$$\bar{R}'_A = \bar{R}_A\,(1-\beta') \tag{3.11'}$$

The total risk of the portfolio net of reserves is

$$\sigma'_A = (1-\beta')\,\sigma_A \tag{3.12}$$

where

$$\sigma_A = \left[\sum\limits_{i=1}^{N}\sum\limits_{j=1}^{N} X_i X_j \sigma_{ij}\right]^{1/2}$$

The expected rate of return (net of reserves) on total available funds is linearly related to the risk of the portfolio

$$\bar{R}'_A = \left(\frac{\bar{R}_A}{\sigma_A}\right)\sigma'_A \tag{3.13}$$

or

$$\left(\frac{\overline{R}_A'}{\sigma_A'}\right) = \left(\frac{\overline{R}_A}{\sigma_A}\right) \tag{3.13'}$$

Equation 3.13' demonstrates that the optimal allocation of available funds net of reserves to each asset $(X_i, \; i = 1, 2, ..., N)$ is unaffected by the reserve constraint β'.

Now suppose that the reserve requirement changes releasing $\Delta\beta'C$ additional funds for investment. Assuming that the firm will actually invest these funds in risky assets, the risk-return trade-off of the investment frontier is then

$$\frac{\Sigma_i \, \Delta\beta'CX_i\overline{R}_i}{[\Sigma_i \, \Sigma_j \, \Delta\beta'CX_i \, \Delta\beta'C \, X_j \, \sigma_{ij}]^{1/2}} = \frac{\Sigma_i \, X_i\overline{R}_i}{[\Sigma_i \, \Sigma_j \, X_iX_j\sigma_{ij}]^{1/2}}$$

which is identical to the trade-off prior to the change in regulation. Hence the optimal allocation of funds (net of reserves) does not change as the constraint is altered. As such, the position and shape of the efficient frontier remains unchanged.

While the allocations of available funds into the frontier portfolios are not affected by reserve requirements, their net effect is to reduce the rate of return on total available funds. As indicated by equation 3.13, the rate of return on *total* available funds falls linearly by the reserve ratio β'. (Specifically, the rate of return on total available funds falls by $\beta'\overline{R}_A$.)

This may be more apparent if we examine the problem in a different way. First, redefine the efficiency locus in terms of total net operating revenue of the portfolio as opposed to rate of return. The position of the efficiency locus in risk and return of revenue space is a function of C (see figure 3-3). Suppose that a reserve requirement is imposed so that the total funds available for investment is reduced by $\beta'C$. This leaves $C' = (1 - \beta')C$ funds available for investment. Given C' funds, the new efficiency locus is $C'C'$. As figure 3-3 indicates, the new locus falls towards the origin.

Now compare portfolio Z on locus CC to portfolio Z' on locus $C'C'$. Portfolio Z' is identical to portfolio Z in the sense that Z' provides the same identical risk-return trade-off as Z. However, portfolio Z' will yield $\beta'R_{TR}$ less revenue on total available funds C. Therefore, the rate of return on the portfolio falls.

Although not a primary focus of this study, it is of interest to examine briefly how a change in reserve requirements may induce an intermediary to reshuffle its portfolio. Suppose an intermediary held portfolio Z on CC prior to reserve regulations (see figure 3-3). After the change in regulation, the firm may select portfolio Z', for instance, which is identical to portfolio Z in terms of risk and return. Accordingly, a change in reserve requirements has had no effect on

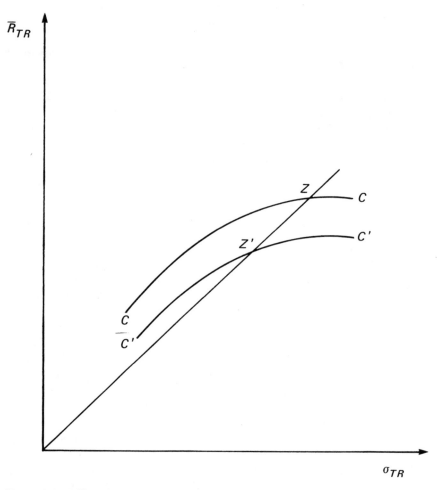

Figure 3-3. Efficient Frontier of Risky Assets in Total Revenue Space: Impact of a Shift in Reserve Requirements

the portfolio choice of the firm and the riskiness of its portfolio per target return. However, the firm may wish to make up for its loss of income by selecting a point past Z' (an income effect).[14] Should this occur, the new portfolio will contain more risky securities than before, and its expected total revenue is less for a given level of portfolio risk. In this case the reserve requirement has indirectly raised the total risk of the firm.

Effects of Portfolio Restrictions on the Profitability
and Risk of Equity Capital of an Intermediary

Before we turn to an analysis of deposit-rate ceilings and capital regulation, it is important to link the effects asset restrictions and reserve requirements have on

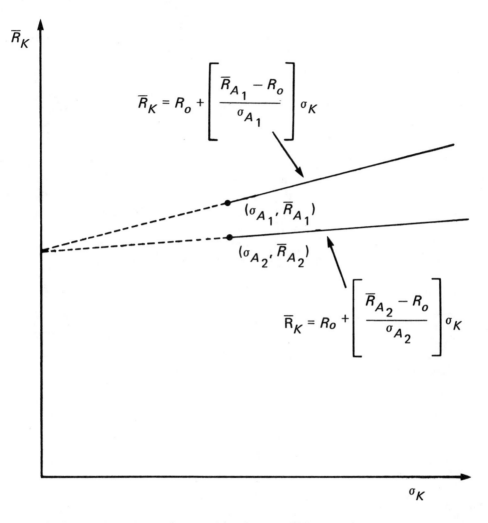

$$\bar{R}_K = R_o + \left[\frac{\bar{R}_{A_1} - R_o}{\sigma_{A_1}} \right] \sigma_K$$

$$(\sigma_{A_1}, \bar{R}_{A_1})$$

$$(\sigma_{A_2}, \bar{R}_{A_2})$$

$$\bar{R}_K = R_o + \left[\frac{\bar{R}_{A_2} - R_o}{\sigma_{A_2}} \right] \sigma_K$$

Note: Each locus is drawn assuming that no deposit-rate ceilings exist and that the intermediary may issue deposits at an unconstrained, market-determined, risk-free rate of interest. The loci differ because of asset restrictions. Asset restrictions reduce the rate of return on total available funds per unit-of-portfolio risk. Thus $\bar{R}_{A_1} > \bar{R}_{A_2}$ for $\sigma_{A_1} = \sigma_{A_2}$, where A_1 and A_2 are the unconstrained and constrained portfolios, respectively.

Figure 3-4. Risk-Return Locus of a Constrained Depository Intermediary Relative to the Unconstrained Locus

the asset portfolio of the firm to the profitability and risk of its capital. This exercise will yield a constrained risk-return locus of an intermediary. Once this locus has been derived, we can compare the constrained risk-return locus to the unconstrained regime.

To begin, define the firm's net rate of return on total available funds before the imposition of reserve requirements as[15]

$$R_N = \frac{\sum_{i=1}^{N} C_i(1 + R_i) - DR_0 - C}{C} \qquad (3.14)$$

$$R_N = R_A - \left(\frac{L}{1 + L}\right) R_0 \qquad (3.14')$$

where

R_o = risk-free rate of interest an intermediary pays for its deposit liabilities prior to Regulation Q ceilings. (*Note:* As discussed in the following section, deposit-rate ceilings reduce the expected average cost of funds below R_o.)

Multiplying equation 3.14 by $(1 + L)$ and taking the expectation yields the expected rate of return on the firm's leveraged equity or reserve capital,

$$\overline{R}_K = (1 + L)\overline{R}_A - LR_o \qquad (3.15)$$

As equation 3.15 indicates, the expected net return to invested capital is a function of the expected return on the portfolio, the degree of leverage, and the price the firm must pay for deposits. Similarly, the risk to equity capital is a function of the risk of the portfolio and the degree of leverage. Thus

$$\sigma_K = (1 + L)\sigma_A \qquad (3.16)$$

Eliminating L from equations 3.15 and 3.16 yields the firm's risk-return locus

$$\overline{R}_K = R_o + \left(\frac{\overline{R}_A - R_o}{\sigma_A}\right)\sigma_K \qquad (3.17)$$

Recall that asset restrictions reduce the expected rate of return on the portfolio $\overline{R}_A$ per unit of portfolio risk σ_A (that is, the constrained frontier falls below the unconstrained frontier). Thus asset restrictions reduce the slope of the intermediary's risk-return locus, which in turn reduces the returns to invested capital per unit of risk it assumes. In risk-return space the constrained, risk-return locus will therefore lie below the unconstrained locus (see figure 3-4).

Reserve requirements also affect an intermediary's profitability and risk; however, reserve requirements do not change the expected return on the portfolio per unit of portfolio risk. Rather, reserve requirements operate so as to raise the cost of borrowed funds and reduce the revenue earned on total available funds, which thereby reduces the returns to invested capital.

Introducing reserve requirements into equations 3.15 and 3.16 yields the following risk-return locus:

$$\overline{R}_K = \frac{R_o}{(1-\beta)} + \left[\frac{R_A(1-\beta) - R_o}{\sigma_A(1-\beta)}\right]\sigma_K \qquad (3.18)$$

As equation 3.18 indicates, the net effect of reserve requirements is to further reduce the slope of the risk-return line. As such, this locus lies below the constrained locus for $\beta = 0$.

Asset restrictions and reserve requirements combine to increase the risk of the asset portfolio and raise the cost of funds to an intermediary. This in turn reduces the profitability and raises the risk to invested capital of the firm. It appears, therefore, that these solvency constraints do not achieve the goal for which they were designed in that equity or reserve capital is exposed to higher risk relative to the unconstrained regime.[16]

Regulation Q Restrictions and Leverage Constraints

In this section we analyze the characteristics of an intermediary's risk-return locus when deposit-rate ceilings and leverage constraints are introduced. Recall that deposit-rate ceilings reduce the average cost of funds to an intermediary. Other factors being equal, these ceilings therefore increase the profitability of the firm. In contrast, leverage constraints reduce the scale of an intermediary. This in turn reduces the return to equity or reserve capital per dollar of capital employed. Combining these regulations with portfolio restrictions yields a complete picture of an intermediary's constrained risk-return locus, and the relative effects of each solvency regulation can then be measured.

In the analysis that follows, we assume that the firm has full control over the total quantity of deposits it holds; however, the mix of deposits and the price the firm must pay for particular categories of deposits are uncertain. This can be explained if the intermediary is a quantity taker in some categories of deposit liabilities (for example, those categories subject to rate ceilings) and a price taker with respect to other categories of deposits (for example, nonregulated CDs). The average cost of funds for a given level of deposits is therefore a random variable that contributes to the risk of equity or reserve capital.

We further assume in this analysis that the firm has only two assets in which it can invest its total available funds. Specifically, an intermediary may invest in either a portfolio of risky assets (specified by regulation) which yields $\widetilde{R}_R$, a risk-free asset which yields R_o, or a combination of the two. This assumption permits us to focus on the effects of rate ceilings and leverage constraints without complicating the analysis unnecessarily with multiple asset categories.

Deposit-rate Ceilings

Before we proceed to the analysis of the constrained risk-return locus of an intermediary, a brief discussion of deposit-rate ceilings is in order. As we discussed in chapters 1 and 2, Regulation Q restrictions specify the maximum rates of interest that intermediaries are permitted to pay for particular types of deposits. These ceilings are generally set below the unconstrained market-determined rate for similar liabilities. An intermediary is permitted, however, to purchase certain deposit liabilities that are not subject to rate ceilings. The rates for these liability categories are determined by the market.

Clearly the firm would prefer that all the deposit liabilities it purchases to be in the form of regulated deposits. However, when this is not possible the firm raises the shortfall by purchasing nonregulated deposits. In this case, the average cost of funds will rise above the rate ceiling but be less than the cost of funds prior to the imposition of deposit-rate ceilings.

At the beginning of each period, an intermediary is unsure of the average and marginal cost of a given level of deposits. On the one hand, the firm is uncertain as to the quantity of funds it can raise from regulated deposit categories. On the other hand, the intermediary is uncertain as to the rate it must pay for nonregulated deposits should a shortfall occur. For any level of total deposits D^*, the uncertain average cost of funds $\tilde{R}_D$ is therefore

$$\tilde{R}_D = \sum_{j=1}^{M} \frac{\tilde{T}_j}{D^*} R_j + \tilde{R}_S \left(\frac{D^* - \Sigma_{j=1} \tilde{T}_j}{D^*} \right) \qquad (3.19)$$

where

T_j = quantity of the jth regulated deposit category (for example, savings deposits).

R_j = rate ceiling for the jth deposit category as specified by Regulation Q. This rate is generally set below the market-determined, risk-free rate R_o.

$\tilde{R}_S$ = market-determined rate on nonregulated deposit liabilities, $R_S \geqslant R_o > R_j \quad j = 1, 2, ..., M.$

D^* = total quantity of deposit liabilities that the firm desires to hold over the period.

For simplicity let us assume only one deposit category is subject to a deposit-rate ceiling. The uncertain average cost of funds is then

$$\tilde{R}_D = \tilde{R}_S + (R_T - \tilde{R}_S)\, \frac{\tilde{T}}{D^*} \tag{3.20}$$

where

R_T = rate ceiling for the single regulated deposit T.

Equation 3.20 indicates that the cost of funds to an intermediary is determined by the quantity of regulated deposits that it can acquire and the price it is obliged to pay for any nonregulated deposits that it must issue. If $T = D^*$, then $R_D = R_T$; the firm is able to raise all its liabilities from regulated deposits, thus its average cost of funds is R_T. Should the firm decide it wants ΔD^* additional deposits, the marginal cost of funds is also R_T if all of ΔD^* can be raised from regulated deposits.

Conversely, if $D^* > T$, then the firm must purchase $D^* - T$ funds at the nonregulated rate R_S. As indicated in equation 3.20, R_D is then greater than R_T. By the same token, any additional funds ΔD^* would have to be purchased at the nonregulated rate. In this case, the marginal cost of funds is R_S.

The ex-ante average cost of funds is determined by the probability that $T \geqslant D^*$ (that is, the supply of regulated deposits is at least equal to the desired level of total deposits). If the probability that $T \geqslant D^*$ is one for a given R_T and D^*, then the expected cost of funds is R_T. However, if this probability is less than 1, then the expected average cost of funds is a function of the joint distribution of T and R_S conditional on R_T (specified by regulation) and D^*.

In general, the expected average cost of funds conditional on R_T, R_S, and D^* is

$$\bar{R}_D\,(R_T,\, R_S,\, D^*) =$$

$$\tag{3.21}$$

$$\int_{D^*}^{\infty} R_T f(T|R_T,\, R_S)\,dT + \int_{0}^{D^*} \frac{R_T T + (D^* - T)}{D^*}\, f(T|R_T,\, R_S)\,dT$$

where

$f(\tilde{T}/R_T,\, R_S)$ = probability distribution of the supply of deposits that is subject to regulation, conditional on R_T and R_S.

Equation 3.21 simply states that the expected average cost of funds to the intermediary depends on the probability that $T \geqslant D^*$.

As we mentioned earlier, R_S is market determined; therefore, R_S is subject to a probability distribution. Assuming R_S and T are correlated, the expected average cost of funds conditional on R_T and D^* only is

$$\bar{R}_D(R_T, D^*) = \int_{-\infty}^{\infty} \int_{D^*}^{\infty} R_T g(T, R_S | R_T) dT dR_S$$

$$+ \int_{-\infty}^{\infty} \int_{0}^{D^*} \frac{R_T T + (D^* - T) R_S}{D^*} g(T, R_S | R_T) dT dR_S$$

(3.22)

where

$g(T, R_S/R_T) =$ joint distribution of the supply of deposits subject to rate regulation and the nonregulated deposit rate, conditional on the deposit-rate ceiling R_T.

Equation 3.22 simply states that the expected cost of funds depends on the joint distribution of the nonregulated deposit rate and the supply of regulated deposits, conditional on the ceiling rate R_T and the quantity of deposits D^* the firm wants to hold.

The variance of the cost of funds can be found by first squaring the arguments in equation 3.22 and integrating the function. Subtracting equation 3.22 squared from this function will yield the variance conditional on R_T and D^*.

The mean and variance of the average cost of funds are a function of R_T and D^*. Thus

$$\bar{R}_D = \bar{R}_D(R_T, D^*)$$
$$\quad\quad (+) \quad (+)$$

(3.23)

and

$$\sigma_{\bar{R}_D}^2 = \sigma_{\bar{R}_D}^2 (R_T, D^*)$$
$$\quad\quad (-) \quad (+)$$

(3.24)

where the signs in parentheses indicate the sign of the derivative of the function with respect to the corresponding variable.

Other factors being equal, an increase in D^* raises $\bar{R}_D$. As an intermediary expands in size, the probability increases that it will experience a shortfall in raising D^* in the form of regulated deposits. Since $R_S > R_T$, additional funds will cost more, raising the average cost of funds. Similarly, the variance of this cost will rise because a larger proportion of total funds is exposed to the uncertain deposit rate R_S. Nonetheless, as long as Regulation Q ceilings are effective and some quantity of funds are raised from regulated deposits, the expected average cost of funds will still be significantly less than $\bar{R}_S$. Indeed, a small increase in D^* may produce only a negligible increase in $\bar{R}_D$ and $\sigma^2_{R_D}$.

The majority of deposit liabilities of a depository intermediary are subject to interest ceilings. Therefore, it is more than likely that an increase in Regulation Q ceilings will lead to an increase in the average cost of funds. Of course, whether the average cost of funds actually rises will depend on the elasticity of the supply of deposits (that is, how the distribution of T shifts with a small change in R_T). In most cases, $\bar{T}$ will rise as R_T rises. Therefore, the firm will be able to acquire a larger percentage of its liabilities in the form of regulated deposits than before. However, the cost of these deposits will be higher as a result of a shift in rate ceilings. This increase will most likely offset any gains that will result from a small decrease in the quantity of nonregulated deposits that would be held by the firm. Specifically, the realized average cost of funds R_D will rise as R_T rises whenever

$$\frac{R_T}{R_S - R_T} > \epsilon_{R_T, T} \qquad (3.25)$$

That is, as long as the inverse of the difference between R_S and R_T as a percent of R_T is greater than $\epsilon_{R_T, T}$, the elasticity of the supply of regulated deposits with respect to the price of these deposits, then $\bar{R}_D$ rises as deposit-rate ceilings rise.[17]

Although the expected average cost of funds will likely rise as deposit-rate ceilings rise, the variance of the cost of funds will most likely fall. Recall that the expected supply of regulated deposits increases as R_T increases. Therefore, the probability that the supply of regulated deposits is at least equal to the desired quantity of total deposits will rise, and the expected quantity of deposits exposed to an uncertain deposit rate will fall.[18]

Moreover, the supply of regulated deposits may become less elastic to changes in R_S as rate ceilings rise. That is, as R_T rises, the difference between the rate ceiling and the nonregulated rate falls. If this difference is less than the transactions cost that depositors must pay to get into nonregulated deposits relative to regulated deposits, then the supply of regulated deposits will become less sensitive to swings in R_S.

Equally important, a rise in deposit-rate ceilings may permit an intermediary to construct a more perfectly hedged asset-liability structure. As we suggested earlier, depository intermediaries may use noninterest-paying devices to attract funds when market rates are above rate ceilings (for example, branches and free checking accounts); that is, intermediaries may make up the differential between R_S and R_T with implicit interest payments. To the extent that these devices are characterized by high fixed costs or generally do not move freely with market-determined interest rates, then the implicit costs of regulated deposits will remain fixed or decline slowly when nonregulated interest rates decline.[19] In contrast, the rate of return on an intermediary's portfolio will track closely market-determined interest rates. Thus as the general level of interest rates fall, the rate of return on the portfolio will fall more rapidly than the cost of funds. The profitability of the firm will therefore decline more sharply than otherwise as interest rates decline. In this case, equity capital may be exposed to lower downside risk when deposit-rate ceilings rise either because noninterest devices will not be required to attract funds or the magnitude of the implicit interest payments made to regulated deposits will fall thereby increasing the flexibility of the firm.

Stated differently, the downside risk of the firm is minimized when the cost of funds and the rate of return on the portfolio move together; that is, when the correlation between the returns to the portfolio and the cost of funds is high. As rate ceilings rise, the use of noninterest devices may either decline or be eliminated permitting the average cost of funds to move freely with open-market interest rates. Therefore, this correlation increases. As such, the total risk of the firm may fall as rate ceilings rise.

The net effect of a change in rate ceilings will depend on how the joint distribution of the supply of regulated deposits T and the nonregulated rate R_S changes. On the one hand, if the expected average cost of funds rises without a commensurate shift in the variance or correlation between the returns to the portfolio and the cost of funds, then the firm is clearly worse off. On the other hand, should the expected cost of funds rise, the variance fall, and the correlation rise, then it is not clear whether the intermediary is better off. The net effect will depend on the relative magnitudes of these shifts (that is, whether the net increase in cost is offset by a reduction in the variance of the cost of funds and an increase in the hedging capabilities of the firm). Accordingly, the effects of a change in deposit-rate ceilings cannot be predicted without first examining the size of these important parameters and the possible magnitudes of change of each parameter under a different regulatory regime. (See chapter 5, which simulates the risk-return locus of an intermediary when all three parameters shift proportionately.)

An intermediary's net return on total available funds subsequent to the imposition of reserve requirements, asset restrictions, and deposit-rate ceilings is

$$R_n = R_o(1 - \beta') + \alpha_R(1 - \beta')(R_R - R_o) - (\frac{L}{1 + L})R_D \qquad (3.26)$$

where

α_R = proportion of total available funds that is invested in the risky portfolio. The term α_R is defined as the investment exposure of an intermediary.

R_o = risk-free rate of return.

R_R = rate of return on the constrained risky portfolio.

R_D = average cost of deposit liabilities.

$L = D^*/K$, defined as the leverage exposure of the firm.

Multiplying equation 3.26 by $(1 + L)$ and taking the expectation yields the expected rate of return on invested capital

$$\bar{R}_K = R_o + \alpha_R(\bar{R}_R - R_o) + L[\alpha_R(\bar{R}_R - R_o)(1 - \beta) + R_o(1 - \beta) - \bar{R}_D] \quad (3.27)$$

Inspection of equation 3.27 indicates that the expected return to capital rises as α_R rises. That is, as the firm invests more of its available funds in the risky portfolio, the ex-ante returns to capital increase. Further, as the firm purchases more deposits per dollar of capital (that is, L rises), the returns to capital also rise.

The risk assumed by equity or reserve capital is

$$\sigma_K = \left[\alpha_R^2 [1 + L(1 - \beta)]^2 \sigma_R^2 + L^2 \sigma_{R_D}^2 - 2\alpha_R [1 + L(1 - \beta)] L\rho \sigma_{R_D} \sigma_R \right]^{1/2} \quad (3.28)$$

where

σ_R^2 = variance of return on the risky portfolio.

ρ = correlation between R_D and R_R.

Equation 3.28 indicates that the risk to capital also rises as both investment exposure and leverage exposure rise. Therefore, as α_R and L increase, both risk and returns to capital increase. Equation 3.28 also indicates that a positive correlation between the cost of funds and the return on the portfolio reduces equity risk. A positive correlation implies that on average the return to the risky portfolio will be high whenever nonregulated deposit rates are high. Therefore, as long as this correlation is significantly greater than zero, an intermediary will not expect its average cost of funds to rise during a period in which the return on the portfolio falls.

Eliminating L from equations 3.27 and 3.28 yields an intermediary's risk-return locus for a given investment exposure α_R

$$R_K = Z + F \sqrt{C \sigma_K^2 - E} \quad (3.29)$$

where

$$A = R_o + \alpha_R (\bar{R}_R - R_o).$$

$$B = \alpha_R \sigma_R \left[\alpha_R \sigma_R (1 - \beta) - \rho \sigma_{R_D} \right].$$

$$C = \sigma_{R_D}^2 - 2\alpha_R (1 - \beta) \rho \sigma_{R_D} \sigma_R + \alpha_R^2 \sigma_{R_D}^2 (1 - \beta)^2.$$

$$E = \alpha_R^2 \sigma_R^2 \sigma_{R_D}^2 (1 - \rho^2).$$

$$F = \left[\alpha_R (\bar{R}_R - R_o)(1 - \beta) + R_o(1 - \beta) - \bar{R}_D \right] / \left[\alpha_R^2 (1 - \beta)^2 \sigma_R^2 + \sigma_{R_D}^2 \right.$$
$$\left. - 2\alpha_R \rho \sigma_R \sigma_{R_D} (1 - \beta) \right].$$

$$Z = A - BF.$$

This locus is a hyperbola in risk-return space with L rising as we move toward larger values of $\bar{R}_K$ and σ_K. Equation 3.29 therefore represents the risk-return trade-off for invested capital of an intermediary subsequent to the imposition of deposit-rate ceilings.

Equation 3.29 displays the effects of deposit-rate ceilings on the risk-return locus. A principal characteristic of this new locus relative to the pre-Regulation Q locus (equation 3.17) is its nonlinearity. A comparison of equations 3.29 and 3.17 will better illustrate the implications of Regulation Q ceilings. Assume that $\beta = 0$ and that an intermediary can borrow all its deposit liabilities at $R_o > \bar{R}_D$. Equation 3.29 then collapses to equation 3.17, the risk-return locus of an intermediary prior to Regulation Q ceilings and reserve requirements. (*Note:* For $\beta \neq 0$, equation 3.29 collapses to equation 3.18.)

Another principal characteristic of the new locus is that it provides returns to capital per unit of risk that are higher relative to those provided under the pre-Regulation Q regime. The reason is straightforward. Deposit-rate ceilings reduce the average cost of funds below R_o, the risk-free borrowing rate. Although Regulation Q ceilings add uncertainty to the average cost of funds, effective ceilings improve the returns to capital.[20] Thus the Regulation Q locus will dominate the pre-Regulation Q locus over the entire range of risk σ_K. In this case, deposit-rate ceilings will partially counteract the adverse effects of portfolio restrictions.

Figure 3-5 presents a graphic display of the comparison. As figure 3-5 indicates, when Regulation Q ceilings are sufficiently low, the Regulation Q constrained locus will dominate the pre-Regulation Q constrained locus at all levels of L. In fact, if Regulation Q ceilings are truly effective, then an intermediary may more than neutralize the adverse effects of portfolio restrictions. That is, the risk-return trade-off may improve to such an extent due to Regulation Q ceilings than an intermediary may offset completely the negative effects of all other regulations.

This may become more apparent if we rearrange equation 3.29:

$$\bar{R}_K = Z + F\sigma_K \sqrt{C - \frac{E}{\sigma_K}} \qquad (3.30)$$

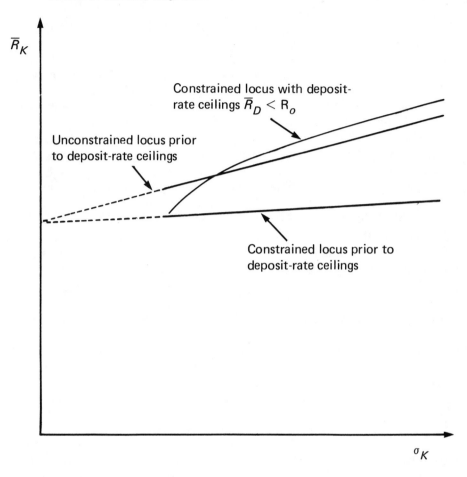

Note: The nonlinear locus depicted here assumes all available funds are invested in the Risky Portfolio.

Figure 3-5. Risk-Return Locus of an Intermediary Before and After the Imposition of Deposit-Rate Ceilings

As σ_K rises (that is, as L rises), holding α_R and $\overline{R}_D$ constant, the equation does not differ a great deal from the linear equation $R_K = Z + F\sigma_K \sqrt{C}$. This linear equation represents the asymptote of the hyperbolic equation 3.29. Thus as an intermediary leverages its equity capital beyond a particular point, its risk-return locus becomes a linear function of σ_K. This implies that the firm will not continually gain increasing returns per unit of risk as it borrows additional funds on each dollar of capital; that is, the risk-return ratio becomes constant.

However, if this limiting ratio is greater than the slope of the unconstrained locus, then a regulated intermediary will be more than compensated for the adverse effects of asset restrictions and reserve requirements (see figure 3-5).

Consequently, Regulation Q ceilings translate into a windfall gain to the regulated intermediary.[21]

Inspection of equations 3.27 and 3.28 indicates that as L rises, both risk and returns to capital rise. That is, as an intermediary acquires more deposits per dollar of capital employed, it moves out along its risk-return locus, equation 3.29. This risk-return locus approaches its asymptote, a linear function of σ_K; thus the risk-return ratio becomes constant. However, as the firm moves out along its locus, it must purchase additional deposits $\Delta D^* = \Delta LK$. Recall that the expected cost of funds and the variance of the cost of funds both rise as D^* rises. As these parameters rise, the risk-return locus will not approach its asymptote; rather, it will begin to fall. In fact, there may be a point on the locus where leverage contributes relatively more risk than return such that the slope of the locus becomes negative. This obtains if an increasing D^* results in raising $\bar{R}_D$ and σ_{R_D} more rapidly than it raises $\bar{R}_K$ per unit of σ_K. Obviously, an intermediary will not move to this point on its locus since it can do much better by simply reducing its scale.

Before we proceed to an analysis of leverage constraints, it is important to point out that the risk-return locus of an intermediary as expressed in equation 3.29 and graphically presented in figure 3-5 is a function of a particular investment exposure α_R. If an intermediary changes the proportion of available funds invested in the risky portfolio, then the position of the risk-return locus will shift. Therefore, a family of loci exist, where the position of each locus is determined by a particular value of α_R.

In general, a single investment exposure will not yield the highest expected return to capital over the entire range of risk σ_K. For example, an intermediary may find that at lower values of risk, its expected return is maximized if it borrows heavily and invests the majority of these funds in the risk-free asset. On the other hand, should the firm select a more risky position on its locus, it may find that the optimal portfolio strategy is to increase its deposits at a decreasing rate and invest the majority of its funds in the risky portfolio. Clearly, the optimal portfolio strategy (that is, the optimal combination of α_R and L) for any level of risk σ_K will depend on the parameters of the joint distribution of R_R and R_D.

An intermediary's efficient risk-return boundary can be found by selecting the combination of α_R and L that maximizes the expected return to capital for a given σ_K. This efficient locus will be the envelope or outer boundary of the set of loci. This locus will have the basic shape and exhibit identical characteristics of each individual locus, but the investment exposure α_R will generally shift as we move along the outer boundary.

Leverage Constraints

Recall from chapter 1 that leverage constraints are typically defined in terms of a capital-asset ratio, namely, $1/1 + L$. Clearly, as L increases, the capital-asset ratio falls. Leverage constraints therefore limit the size of L.

Let the leverage constraint imposed by regulation be L_{max}. Substituting L_{max} into equation 3.29 reveals that capital regulation reduces the portion of the locus on which an intermediary may operate. Thus the maximum risk and return combination the firm may select is determined by L_{max} (figure 3-6 illustrates this graphically).

In general, asset restrictions, reserve requirements, and deposit-rate ceilings determine the shape and position of an intermediary's risk-return locus. On the other hand, regulation of capital limits the portion of the locus that is available to an intermediary regardless of its position in risk-return space. As the leverage constraint shifts, the operating area of an intermediary shifts correspondingly without changing the basic position or shape of the locus.

It is important to note that if the leverage constraint is set too low, an intermediary may not be able to take advantage of its "cheap" deposits to the extent necessary to neutralize the adverse effects of portfolio restrictions. For example, the leverage constraint may be so severe that the portion of the risk-return locus the firm is permitted to operate on may be below the

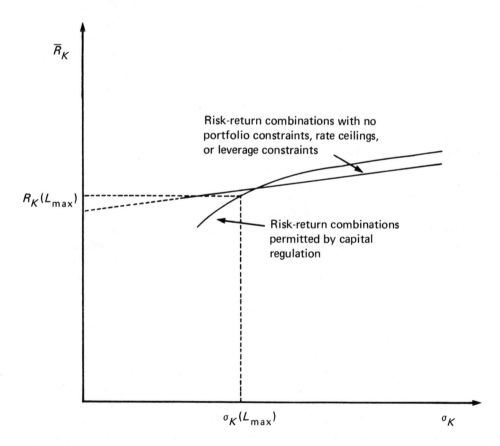

Figure 3-6. Risk-Return Locus of an Intermediary Subject to a Leverage Constraint

unconstrained locus leveraged at the riskless rate $R_o > \bar{R}_D$ (see figure 3-6). Consequently, an intermediary will be unable to offset the impact of asset restrictions.

Although a leverage constraint does not affect the basic shape and position of the risk-return locus generated for a given investment exposure, it does so to a portion of the efficient risk-return boundary. Recall that the efficient boundary is found by maximizing the returns to capital with respect to α_R and L, for a given risk σ_K. This boundary can be found in a similar fashion when a leverage constraint is introduced; yet this constraint must be satisfied for any value of σ_K (that is, $L^* \leqslant L_{max}$). Obviously, as long as the optimal value of L is less than or equal to L_{max}, the constraint has no effect. However, when the optimal value of L is greater than L_{max}, then the firm must select a different combination of α_R and L such that the constraint is satisfied and the return to capital is maximized. This will leave a portion of the efficient boundary below the previously unconstrained efficient boundary.

The net impact of a leverage constraint is to reduce the area in which an intermediary may operate. The firm may be able to trade off investment exposure with leverage exposure so that it can expand its operating area; yet this may extend the locus only slightly. Interestingly, a leverage constraint does not increase the riskiness of the intermediary per se (with the exception of the portion of the boundary where the firm suboptimally trades off leverage exposure for investment exposure); rather the regulation reduces the number of combinations of risk and return that is available to the firm.

Interrelationship between Solvency Regulation and the Existence of Depository Intermediaries

The preceding discussion illustrated how the position, basic shape, and operating portion of an intermediary's risk-return locus are largely determined by the parameters of solvency regulation (see equation 3.29). Accordingly, as any one parameter changes, the characteristics of the efficient boundary will change. Recall from chapter 2 that each type of depository intermediary is subject to different solvency parameters or standards. Therefore, the risk-return locus of each type of depository intermediary will differ.

Given the respective values of each solvency parameter, one type of intermediary may enjoy a superior opportunity locus relative to others. For example, if one type of intermediary is permitted by regulation to invest in a broader category of assets than its counterparts, then it may provide its owners a higher risk-adjusted return than the other intermediaries.

A superior risk-return locus will provide the favored intermediary a significant advantage in attracting new capital. In general, capital will flow toward those intermediaries that earn a superior risk-adjusted rate of return on their capital and flow from those intermediaries that suffer from particularly restrictive solvency regulations. The flows of capital will continue until the rates of return earned by each type of depository intermediary are equalized.

Equality of risk-adjusted returns can occur whenever a significant number of new firms can enter the market in which superior returns are earned and/or a significant number of old firms leave the market in which inferior returns are earned. This exit and entry of firms should normally continue until the risk-adjusted rates of return are equal across all markets. However, each type of intermediary is somewhat protected from competition by branching laws and charter requirements. Nonetheless, if any one type of intermediary cannot generate the risk-adjusted return that is being earned elsewhere, then it will not grow and will ultimately decline.

On the other hand, regulators can react to a declining intermediary and stop the flow of capital to a certain extent by relaxing the solvency regulations that inordinately restrict its profitability. This would seem to be the appropriate strategy; yet regulators must ensure that they give neither advantage nor disadvantage to any one type of intermediary.

A depository intermediary must also compete with an unconstrained intermediary (say, a mutual fund) for new investors.[22] A mutual fund can offer an investor a widely diversified portfolio that is not subject to the same asset restrictions that most depository intermediaries must satisfy. Nonetheless, a mutual fund cannot hold an identical set of assets that a depository intermediary can hold. Consequently, the characteristics of their portfolios may differ from those of each type of depository intermediary.[23]

For the sake of comparison, let us assume that a private investor has the opportunity to invest in either a mutual fund that holds an unconstrained, widely diversified portfolio or a depository intermediary that is subject to asset restrictions and reserve requirements. If both types of intermediaries can borrow at the risk-free rate R_o, then it is not clear which type of intermediary will offer a higher risk-adjusted return on invested capital.

Clearly, an unconstrained intermediary will provide a superior return if its portfolio contains assets that have identical characteristics to those held by a depository intermediary. In this case, a depository intermediary could not compete for capital and would ultimately be forced from the market.

Conversely, if the composition of the unconstrained intermediary's portfolio differs significantly from the portfolio of a depository intermediary, then it is not clear whether any one firm has an advantage in attracting new investors. Nonetheless, asset restriction will make the depository intermediary riskier than otherwise resulting in an inefficient use of deposit funds and investors' capital.

As we discussed earlier, Regulation Q ceilings may improve the risk-return locus of a depository intermediary. Indeed, the Regulation Q locus may rise above the unconstrained locus, thereby offsetting completely the effects of asset restrictions and reserve requirements. In this case a constrained depository intermediary will be able to compete effectively with an unconstrained intermediary that is unable to raise funds at similar rates. In fact, if the constrained intermediary is able to raise funds at rates that more than compensate for the effects of all other regulations, then its owners will immediately realize a windfall gain as the value of the firm shifts to capitalize these favorable rate ceilings. Obviously, this gain will ultimately be eliminated as new firms are permitted to enter the market.

Even though the preceding comparisons made are somewhat artificial, they do illustrate an important factor that must be considered in evaluating the impacts of regulation—namely, if solvency regulations are inordinately severe, then the depository intermediary industry will have difficulty attracting new capital. This will in the long run force the more restricted intermediaries to leave the market. Their leaving in turn will reduce the quantity of services provided to both lenders and borrowers, thereby reducing economic growth and real output.

To evaluate properly the costs and benefits of solvency regulation, a comparison of risk-return characteristics must be made between a nonregulated depository intermediary and the present depository intermediaries with their respective regulations. This comparison will not only yield insight into the absolute effects of solvency regulation relative to the unconstrained regime but will also provide a much needed comparison of the relative effects of regulation across each type of intermediary. We now turn to these comparisons in the following chapters.

Summary

A depository intermediary's risk-return locus (that is, the optimal set of risk and return combinations) is affected by each major solvency instrument in the following ways: (1) Asset restrictions constrain an intermediary from investing in the most favorable and efficient combination of risky assets. Therefore, the return from the portfolio is less for any level of portfolio risk. This in turn increases the risk of capital over the entire risk-return locus (that is, the locus shifts down in risk-return space). (2) Reserve requirements reduce the quantity of funds available for investment. While reserve requirements do not affect the optimal allocation of funds to the portfolio, they do reduce the returns to capital for any level of risk. Consequently, the locus shifts down in risk-return space. (3) Regulation Q ceilings reduce the average cost of funds to an intermediary, thereby increasing its profitability; that is, deposit-rate ceilings enable an intermediary to leverage its invested capital at a below-market interest rate. Accordingly, the risk-return locus will rise, offsetting to a certain extent, the effects of portfolio restrictions. On the other hand, deposit-rate ceilings may increase the variance of the average cost of funds and reduce the flexibility of the firm. Consequently, the variance of the cost of funds may be greater in a Regulation Q regime than in a regime where intermediaries must purchase all deposits at market-determined rates. Therefore, as rate ceilings rise, the average cost of funds will rise, but the variance of the cost of funds may fall. The net effect of Regulation Q restrictions on the risk-return locus is therefore ambiguous and must be measured empirically. And (4) leverage constraints do not, in general, affect the riskiness of the intermediary per se (that is, capital regulation does not shift the locus); rather, these constraints specify an area of the locus on which an intermediary may operate. However, if these constraints are too restrictive, then a depository intermediary may not be able to take advantage of "cheap" deposits to the extent required to neutralize the adverse effects of portfolio restrictions. Consequently, an intermediary may earn less on its capital than may indeed be required by its investors, and capital will flow from the firm.

It should be noted again that the comparisons made in the text between the pre- and post-Regulation Q loci were somewhat artificial in that the pre-Regulation Q locus was based on the assumption that the firm could raise all of its deposits at the risk-free rate of interest. This simplification was utilized primarily to focus attention on the effects of Regulation Q restrictions and leverage constraints. A more appropriate comparison would, of course, be between an unconstrained intermediary that must raise its deposits at the market-determined rate R_S and the constrained intermediary that enjoys the benefits of Regulation Q ceilings (see chapter 5 for such a comparison).

It should be clear from the discussion and the basic relationships presented that each solvency regulation cannot be evaluated for its full impact without treating all solvency instruments simultaneously. As our simple model indicates, regulators cannot know a priori at what level each regulatory parameter should be set such that the firm has neither an advantage nor a disadvantage in the market for capital. Further, regulators cannot know without analyzing all solvency instruments simultaneously, which instruments best reduce the probability of insolvency (see chapter 6).

To better understand the trade-offs that may exist among regulations, chapters 4 and 5 present an empirical examination of the effects of each solvency instrument across each type of depository intermediary in light of the other parameters of regulation. These chapters focus on the investment opportunity set and risk-return characteristics of each type of intermediary. Chapter 6 then translates these findings into a measure of the probability of insolvency.

Notes

1. A discussion of this point is found on pages 50-54.

2. See J. Mingo and B. Wolkowitz, "The Effects of Regulation on Bank Portfolios, Capital and Profitability," in *Conference on Bank Structure and Competition* (Chicago: Federal Reserve Bank of Chicago, 1974), pp. 47-58, and M.F. Koehn and A.M. Santomero, "Regulation of Bank Capital and Portfolio Risk," for a discussion of how intermediaries may react to changes in particular regulatory parameters.

3. The assumption that intermediaries control the level of total deposits is well known in the literature. See, for example, D. Pyle, "On the Theory of Financial Intermediation," *Journal of Finance* 26 (1971):737-747. This assumption implies that management is unsure of the price it must pay to hold a given

level of total deposits. Thus the total cost of funds is uncertain as opposed to the total quantity of deposits.

4. See O. Hart and D. Jaffee, "On the Application of Portfolio Theory to Depository Financial Intermediaries," *Review of Economic Studies* 41 (1974):129-147; and J. Michaelson and R. Goshay, "Portfolio Selection in Financial Intermediaries: A New Approach," *Journal of Financial and Quantitive Analysis* 2 (1967):166-199, which use risk-averse utility maximization to describe the behavior of intermediaries. See J. Cozzolino and T. Taga, "On the Separability of Corporate Stockholders' Risk Preferences," mimeographed (Philadelphia, Pa.: University of Pennsylvania, 1976), for a rigorous justification of this approach.

5. In a strict sense, a mean-standard-deviation assumption implies either that preferences are quadratic or that the probability distributions of returns are normal. For example, regardless of the utility function used to represent the risk preferences of the firm, if returns are normally distributed, then expected utility is a function strictly of mean and standard deviation. In general, however, an investment decision based only on the mean and standard deviation of returns provides a fair approximation to the optimal decision under relatively robust conditions. See S.C. Tsiang, "The Rationale of the Mean-Standard Deviation Analysis, Skewness Preference, and the Demand for Money," *American Economic Review* 62 (1972):354-371. It is important to recognize that the standard deviation of returns to capital is the appropriate measure of risk within the context of this analysis as opposed to covariance of earnings, which has been identified as the appropriate risk measure in the setting of the Capital Asset Pricing Model (CAPM). Recall that a major concern to both regulators and owners is the probability of failure (that is, the total risk of the firm). Owners/managers are of course concerned with loss of capital. Regulators, on the other hand, are concerned with the social cost associated with the failure of an intermediary. In either case, the total risk of the firm becomes a focal point. As we will show in chapter 6, the probability of failure of the firm is principally determined by the standard deviation of earnings. Therefore, even if the CAPM framework were valid, within this context the standard deviation of returns becomes important, not just the covariance of earnings. See J. Mingo, "Regulation of Financial Institutions: An Overview," in *Evaluation of the Social Impact of Regulation,* pp. 416-468, for a more in-depth discussion of this point. See J. Tobin, "Liquidity Preferences and Behavior Towards Risk," *Review of Economic Studies* 25 (1958):65-85, for arguments supporting the mean-standard-deviation approach. For a criticism of this approach, see G. Hanock and H. Levy, "The Efficiency Analysis of Choices Involving Risk," *Review of Economic Studies* 36 (1969):335-346.

6. An implication of competitive markets for an intermediary is that it does not influence the prevailing set of interest rates. That is, an intermediary is sufficiently small relative to the rest of the market that its decision will have little impact on prices and quantities. As pointed out by Rubinstein, "Competi-

tion and Approximation," *The Bell Journal of Economics* 9 (1978):280-286, the assumption of competitive markets does not mean necessarily that individual consumers or firms have no influence over the prevailing prices or interest rates but rather that they behave as if this were true.

7. J.A. James, "Portfolio Selection with an Imperfect Competitive Asset Market," *Journal of Financial and Quantitative Analysis* 11 (1976):831-846, snows that the effect of monopoly position in one market does not change the basic characteristics of the efficient frontier.

8. A general equilibrium model of the capital markets that includes intermediaries and adequately treats the issues of regulation has not yet been developed. Certainly the CAPM is inappropriate in this setting given several assumptions of the model. For example, (1) the CAPM assumes no transactions cost and a frictionless market and (2) the quantity of all assets in the market opportunity set is assumed to be fixed during the period. Obviously if these assumptions held, there would indeed be no reason for intermediaries to exist. Until we fully understand the pricing of financial assets in a world of segmented markets and transaction costs, we must base our analysis on the assumption that intermediary management invokes its own risk preferences when leverage and investment decisions are made. As mentioned in the text, since the size of the institutions in question is small, this assumption does not appear to be unrealistic.

9. The efficient frontier is made up of portfolios with maximum expected return for all possible levels of risk. For an extensive discussion of the efficient frontier, see R. Merton, "An Analytical Derivation of the Efficient Portfolio Frontier," *Journal of Financial and Quantitative Analysis* 7 (1972):1851-1872. The original development of this model is, of course, from H.M. Markowitz, *Portfolio Selection* (New York: Wiley, 1959).

10. *Functional Cost Analysis* (Washington, D.C.: Board of Governors of the Federal Reserve System) uses this definition for total available funds.

11. The implication of a singular variance-covariance matrix is that the return on one asset is a linear combination of returns of the other assets. Nonsingularity is required if we are to derive a unique solution to the optimal proportions held of each asset in each efficient portfolio. See M. Mossin, *Theory of Financial Markets* (Englewood Cliffs, N.J.: Prentice-Hall, 1973), pp. 53-56. Note that we can be assured of nonsingularity by simply aggregating individual assets to form asset bundles that retain the basic characteristics of the underlying assets.

12. See W.F. Sharpe, *Portfolio Theory and Capital Markets* (New York: McGraw-Hill, 1970), pp. 62-73, for a thorough discussion of the effect short-sell constraints and quantity restrictions have on the efficient frontier.

13. Some quantity constraints are defined in terms of total available funds. For example, 80 percent of an S&L's portfolio must be invested in mortgages. This constraint can be expressed as $\Sigma_{d=1}^{M} X_j \geq 0.80$, where M is the total number of mortgages in the portfolio.

14. C.J. Prestopino, "The Impact of Differential Reserve Requirements," examines the response of a commercial bank to changes in reserve requirements. Prestopino tests empirically whether banks shift into riskier securities as reserve requirements go up, that is, an income effect. He also tests whether an increase in reserves produces a liquidity effect whereby banks are more willing to increase the size of their loan portfolios.

15. To determine the effects asset restrictions and reserve requirements have on the profitability and risk of capital, we will assume that the firm is able to purchase all its deposit liabilities at an unconstrained, market-determined, risk-free rate of interest R_o. This occurs, of course, prior to Regulation Q ceilings. Clearly, the borrowing rate R_o is riskless for only those deposit liabilities that mature at the end of the portfolio horizon. If deposit liabilities mature prior to the end of the period or if the firm cannot raise all the deposits it desires at the rate R_o, then the firm would be unsure of the cost of a given level of total deposits. Regulation Q ceilings and the uncertain cost of funds is discussed extensively in the next section.

16. The results somewhat overstate the unwanted effects of reserves, principally because we assumed the firm could purchase any quantity of deposits it desired at the risk-free rate R_o. Clearly, if deposit levels were random, then the firm would willingly hold some assets in cash to protect against unexpected withdrawals. Nonetheless, the analysis does indicate that reserve requirements can actually increase the risk of the firm.

17. For example, if $R_S = 1.44$ and $R_T = 1.30$, then $\epsilon_{R_T, T}$ must be greater than 9.3 before the average cost of funds will fall when rate ceilings rise.

18. Essentially the firm expects that a larger proportion of funds will be subject to the fixed rate R_T. Although the firm may not actually realize a shift to more regulated deposits, on average we would expect this to be so. Consequently, a smaller proportion of funds must be raised at the uncertain rate R_S.

19. See E.J. Kane, "Getting Along Without Regulation Q: Testing the Standard View of Deposit-rate Competition During the 'Wild Card Experiment,' " *Journal of Finance* 33 (1978):921-932.

20. This comparison is introduced only for heuristic purposes. Its presentation is not meant to imply that a firm can select the regime in which it operates. It is presented solely as a means to highlight the unique characteristics of Regulation Q. The significance of Regulation Q can be seen in comparing its effects on the risk of the firm to those introduced when an intermediary purchases all its funds at the uncertain market-determined rate $\tilde{R}_S$. This comparison is presented and discussed in chapter 5.

21. An implication of deposit-rate ceilings, of secondary importance here, is that disintermediation occurs as a function of conflicting regulatory effects. In this case disintermediation is indicated by a firm sliding down its risk-return locus. It does so when it loses unregulated deposits and is unable to raise the short-fall through nonregulated deposits.

22. A depository intermediary must compete with all types of industries for new capital, not just other intermediaries. The comparison made in the text is presented primarily to highlight the effects of solvency regulation.

23. The question does arise why the owners of a depository intermediary would care whether the firm maintains a diversified portfolio. Certainly in the absence of transactions costs and market imperfections, a stockholder would be indifferent to or insist that the firm not hold a diversified portfolio. But, of course, under these conditions there would be no basic reason for intermediaries to exist. Accordingly, we must attribute the existence of intermediaries to their access to better information about investment opportunities and their lower transactions costs. Competition among intermediaries for new investors should thus focus on the extent to which each type of institution can provide a well-diversified portfolio to its owners with minimal transactions costs. Clearly, those firms that are subject to little or no asset restrictions can maintain a well-diversified portfolio for a lower price (they have lower operating or search costs) than those that are more severely constrained. Also, as we discussed earlier, asset restrictions eliminate significant opportunities for diversification.

4

Sources and Description of Data

Chapter 3 discussed how each type of solvency instrument affects the risk and profitability of a depository intermediary.[1] It also discussed how these instruments interact to determine the position, basic shape, and operating area of the risk-return locus. The analysis demonstrated how solvency regulation may increase the risk of a regulated intermediary relative to an unregulated firm. Accordingly, regulation may not achieve the goal of ensuring the solidity of the industry as originally designed. As a further consequence, because regulation may unfavorably shift an intermediary's risk-return locus relative to the unconstrained sector, the industry as a whole may be severely handicapped in its bid for capital and its ability to grow. This in turn will produce economic distortions reducing total output in society.

The characteristics of the constrained risk-return locus depend on the parameters of the joint distribution of portfolio returns and the cost of funds and the standards of regulation. Therefore, it is not possible to capture analytically the full effects of each regulatory constraint. Although we can examine the impact each solvency instrument has on equations 3.27 and 3.28 and then trace these effects to the efficient locus, it is not possible to measure the absolute effects of regulation relative to the unconstrained regime and the relative effects across all types of depository intermediaries. Accordingly, an empirical analysis is necessary to estimate the full consequence of solvency regulation.

The empirical analysis presented in the following chapter provides an estimate of the size and extent of the consequences of regulation. This analysis also provides an estimate of the effects that may result from a small shift in each solvency standard.

For example, it has often been suggested that a depository intermediary is exposed to higher risk as a result of Regulation Q ceilings (see chapter 3 for a discusssion of this issue). That is, although a firm will enjoy a lower average cost of funds, it may be accepting greater variance of the cost of funds as a result. It has further been suggested that several types of intermediaries may have an unfair advantage in attracting deposits since deposit-rate ceilings differ across intermediaries. Therefore, Regulation Q ceilings should either be relaxed or eliminated.[2] However, recall from chapter 3 that the effects of a change in rate ceilings are ambiguous and depend on the relative shift of the important parameters of the joint distribution of the supply of regulated deposits and the nonregulated deposit rate. Clearly, without an empirical examination of the possible changes in these parameters, the consequence of changing or eliminating Regulation Q ceilings cannot be predicted accurately.

This chapter presents single-period estimates of the means and variances/ covariances of rates of return (or holding-period yields) for a reasonable "universe" of financial assets. Because the relevant expected rates of return to intermediaries are net of operating costs (that is, acquisition and servicing costs) and expected losses, the rate of return of each asset is constructed net of these factors. This chapter also presents estimates of the important solvency standards currently in effect for each intermediary. Since each type of intermediary differs in purpose and regulatory agency, the current set of regulatory standards vary widely (see chapter 2). Both sets of data provide the information necessary to carry out the empirical analysis of the effects of regulation.

Recall that the two-parameter model is rigorously justified when either the decision maker's risk preferences are quadratic or the distribution of return is normal. Since the quadratic utility function may be too restrictive, the sample distributions of returns must be tested to determine whether the assumption of normality is justified.[3] To test for normality, the Studentized Range Test was used.[4] This test is sensitive to extreme observations that indicate whether the underlying distributions have "fat tails." The Studentized Range Test will therefore indicate whether there is too high a probability of observing extremely high or low values than would be observed if the sample rates of return were drawn from a normal distribution.

Once the means and variances/covariances are presented, a brief discussion of these statistics follows. Then the current set of regulatory standards are estimated and the results are reported. Our estimates of the effects of solvency regulation on each type of intermediary are presented in chapter 5.

Ex-post Rates of Return on Assets

Because the model presented in chapter 3 is based on a single-period portfolio horizon, single-period rates of return must be constructed. In this study the portfolio horizon extends over one quarter of a year.

The collection of assets included in the "universe" of feasible investments are presented in table 4-1. As the table indicates, the "universe" includes a variety of U.S. Treasury bill and bond indices, corporate bond indices, municipal bond indices, commercial and consumer loans, mortgage loans, and an industrial equity index.

The bond indices cover various maturities and quality. The bond data derive from bond indices of yield to maturity, which are compiled by Standard and Poors. These indices were converted to a price index so that a rate of return could be calculated; a particular coupon rate was assumed for each type of bond.[5]

Table 4-1
Universe of Financial Assets
(Quarterly Observations)

	$\bar{R}_i(\%)$	$\sigma_i(\%)$
	(Net of Expected Costs and Losses)	
Risky Assets		
A1[a] U.S. government discount bill: 6 months	1.37	0.438
A2[a] U.S. government discount bill: 12 months	1.66	0.988
A3 U.S. government 20-year/3% bond: 3.5 years	1.61	2.360
A4 U.S. government 20-year/3% bond: 7.5 years	1.64	3.270
A5 Short-term business loan: 90-day discount	1.38	0.447
A6 Commercial loan: 4 years amortized	1.67	2.099
A7[a] Other consumer loan: 24 months amortized	1.91	0.192
A8[a] Mobile home loan: 84 months amortized	1.57	0.815
A9[a] Automobile loan: 36 months amortized	1.45	0.374
A10[a] Personal consumer loan: 12 months amortized	1.94	0.361
A11[a] FHLBB mortgage: 26 years amortized	1.50	2.887
A12 FHA mortgage: 30 years amortized	1.86	4.940
A13[a] Aaa composite 20-year/4% bond: 1 year	1.27	0.956
A14[a] Aaa composite 20-year/4% bond: 10 year	1.40	2.763
A15 Aaa composite 20-year/4% bond: 20 year	1.46	3.994
A16[a] Baa composite 20-year/4% bond: 1 year	1.49	7.218
A17[a] Baa composite 20-year/4% bond: 10 year	1.52	3.679
A18 Baa composite 20-year/4% bond: 20 year	1.82	6.179
A19 Aaa municipal 20-year/4% bond: 1 year	1.80	0.558
A20 Aaa municipal 20-year/4% bond: 10 year	2.14	4.663
A21 Aaa municipal 20-year/4% bond: 20 year	1.56	6.050
A22 Baa municipal 20-year/4% bond: 1 year	1.96	0.453
A23[a] Baa municipal 20-year/4% bond: 10 year	1.66	4.013
A24 Baa municipal 20-year/4% bond: 20 year	2.42	5.740
A25[a] Industrial equity index	2.75	8.236
Riskless Asset		
A26 U.S. government discount bill: 3 months	1.44	

Sources: Rates of return for asset categories A1, A2, and A5-A12 were constructed from data appearing in various issues of the *Federal Reserve Bulletin*. Rates of return for asset categories A3, A4 and A13-A25 were constructed from data appearing in *Standard and Poor's Trade and Securities Statistics Security Price Index Record* (New York: Standard and Poor's, 1977).

[a]An asset that has a sample rate-of-return distribution that was not rejected as being generated from a normal distribution (.05 significance level or less).

To calculate the rates of return of each asset for each period, a price or capital value of the asset was calculated for the beginning and end of the period. Interest or dividends, operating expense, and losses are then added to the change in price to calculate the rate of return. Thus

$$R_t = \frac{P_t - P_{t-1}}{P_{t-1}} + \frac{I_t}{P_{t-1}} - \frac{E_t}{P_{t-1}} - \frac{Lo_t}{P_{t-1}}$$

where

R_t = sample rate of return in period t.

P_t = price or capital value of an asset at the end of period t.

I_t = quarterly interest or dividend payment for period t.

E_t = acquisition and service costs over period t.

Lo_t = dollar default over period t.[6]

This calculation was made for each quarter from 1969 to 1977 inclusively.[7] Thus rate of return data were generated for 36 quarters.[8]

It is important to mention that "yield to maturity" was not used to measure rates of return on bonds. Clearly, given the purchase price, the yield on any bond is fixed over the maturity period. However, a bond's rate of return over a single period is a random variable as interest rates fluctuate and bond prices change. In addition, the "annual percentage rate" was not used to measure rates of return on amortized loans.[9] Because payments received over the period will include part of the amortized principal, the capital value of a loan will change over the period whenever loan rates change and part of the balance of the loan is taken down.

The rate-of-return estimates for each asset include realized and unrealized capital gains or losses to the firm. As we mentioned in chapter 3, a shift in the capital value of each asset represents either an opportunity loss or gain to the equity holders and therefore should be included in the rate-of-return calculations.

The point estimate of the mean rate of return for each category of asset was calculated as a simple arithmetic average of the quarterly returns[10]

$$\bar{R}_i = \frac{1}{36} \sum_{t=1}^{36} R_{it}, \quad i = 1, 2, ..., 25$$

where

R_{it} = rate of return on the ith asset for the sample period t.

$\bar{R}_i$ = arithmetic average. Note we use the same notation previously used to represent the expectation operator.

The point estimate of the covariance of returns on investment i and j and variance of returns for $i = j$ were calculated as follows

$$\bar{\sigma}_{ij} = \frac{1}{36} \sum_{t=1}^{36} (R_{it} - \bar{R}_{it})(R_{jt} - \bar{R}_{jt}), \quad i, j = 1, 2, ..., 25$$

Table 4-1 presents the means and variances of the rate-of-return distributions. Table 4-2 presents the correlations across all assets.[11]

The data in table 4-1 indicate that the average rate of return is an increasing function of risk (standard deviation). Thus a low rate of return is associated generally with a low standard deviation. (Note that the highest average rate of return has the highest standard deviation, namely the industrial equity index.) Although this relationship is not consistent for every mean return and standard deviation, casual observation of the data tends to support the general proposition that investors require a higher return to accept a higher risk. However, it is well known that the covariance properties of an asset significantly contribute to the risk of a portfolio. Thus the mean as a simple function of its standard deviation will most likely not capture the complete risk-return relationship.

The correlations presented in table 4-2 indicate that substantial risk reduction can occur if a portfolio is constructed from the entire "universe" of assets. This is due to the absence of perfect positive correlation between assets. As is well known, imperfect correlations between assets will provide for risk reduction when a portfolio is formed with those assets. However, some correlations in the matrix are quite high and positive (for example, the correlation of A3 and A4). Yet both of these assets are government bonds with identical coupon rates; consequently, it should not be surprising that their rates of return tend to move in unison. In general, however, preliminary review of the data seem to indicate that enlarging the universe of alternative investments will improve an intermediary's risk-return investment frontier and therefore its risk-return locus. We will address this issue in detail in the following chapter.

Estimates of the Regulatory Standards

In order to estimate the effects of regulation across all types of depository intermediaries, the current effective standards or parameters of regulation for each intermediary must first be estimated. These standards were determined as follows:

1. The reserve requirement β is a weighted average of the relevant set of reserve or liquidity requirements; the weights are determined by the mix of deposits actually held by each type of intermediary.[12] Thus the effective reserve requirements are determined by the following equation

$$\beta = \sum_{i=1}^{M} \beta_i \left(\frac{D_i}{D^*} \right)$$

where

β_i = reserve requirement imposed on the ith deposit type.

D_i/D^* = proportion of total deposits held in the ith deposit type.[13]

Table 4-2
Correlation Matrix of Rates of Return

	A1	A2	A3	A4	A5	A6	A7	A8	A9	A10	A11	A12	A13
A1	1.00	0.79[a]	0.51[a]	0.40[a]	0.64[a]	0.33[a]	0.00	-0.12	-0.03	0.21	-0.22	0.17	0.32[a]
A2		1.00	0.61[a]	0.52[a]	0.67[a]	0.48[a]	0.04	-0.09	-0.13	0.13	-0.26	0.28[a]	0.39[a]
A3			1.00	0.91[a]	0.23	0.45[a]	-0.20	0.42	-0.04	-0.21	-0.09	0.62[a]	0.38[a]
A4				1.00	0.21	0.51[a]	-0.23[a]	0.15	-0.02	-0.32[a]	-0.08	0.66[a]	0.40[a]
A5					1.00	0.42[a]	0.26	-0.27[a]	-0.21	0.10	-0.40[a]	0.03	0.25
A6						1.00	-0.20	0.32[a]	0.12	0.39[a]	0.25	0.61[a]	0.46[a]
A7							1.00	0.08	0.07	0.56[a]	-0.19	-0.25	-0.30[a]
A8								1.00	0.27[a]	-0.17	0.38[a]	0.21	-0.07
A9									1.00	-0.12	0.31[a]	0.29[a]	-0.20
A10										1.00	0.41[a]	-0.39[a]	-0.37[a]
A11											1.00	0.40	0.10
A12												1.00	0.30
A13													1.00

	A14	A15	A16	A17	A18	A19	A20	A21	A22	A23	A24	A25
A1	0.04	0.26	0.07	0.09	0.11	0.40[a]	0.28[a]	0.16	0.23	0.18	0.18	0.03
A2	0.20	0.30[a]	0.19	0.03	0.22	0.39[a]	0.33[a]	0.20	0.13	0.21	0.17	0.07
A3	0.49[a]	0.72[a]	0.41[a]	0.47[a]	0.61[a]	0.54[a]	0.58[a]	0.63[a]	0.33[a]	0.55[a]	0.58[a]	0.17
A4	0.56[a]	0.76[a]	0.44[a]	0.45[a]	0.70[a]	0.59[a]	0.67[a]	0.74[a]	0.33[a]	0.59[a]	0.69[a]	0.27[a]
A5	-0.04	-0.14	-0.01	-0.34[a]	-0.18	0.15	0.00	-0.18	0.01	-0.20	-0.21	-0.20
A6	0.15	0.43[a]	0.22	0.17	0.43[a]	0.22	0.33[a]	0.20	0.16	0.12	0.22	0.44[a]
A7	-0.32[a]	-0.34[a]	-0.22	-0.26	-0.36[a]	-0.18	-0.22	-0.27[a]	-0.17	-0.14	-0.22	-0.24[a]
A8	0.22	0.23	0.06	0.21	0.90	0.19	0.10	0.22	0.20	0.20	0.24[a]	0.56[a]
A9	0.11	0.89	0.20	0.35[a]	0.14	0.22	0.05	0.16	0.07	-0.16	0.09	0.39[a]
A10	-0.38[a]	-0.47[a]	-0.28	-0.35[a]	-0.36[a]	0.10	-0.18	-0.22	-0.03	-0.07	-0.23	-0.41[a]
A11	0.21	0.28	0.25	0.55[a]	0.26	-0.06	0.11	0.05	0.00	0.03	0.01	0.55[a]
A12	0.52[a]	0.67[a]	0.49[a]	0.61[a]	0.74[a]	0.44[a]	0.64[a]	0.53[a]	0.11	0.29[a]	0.48[a]	0.49[a]
A13	0.22	0.46[a]	0.03	0.17	0.37[a]	-0.10	0.47[a]	0.40[a]	0.06	0.18	0.33[a]	0.02

Table 4-2 continued

	A14	A15	A16	A17	A18	A19	A20	A21	A22	A23	A24	A25
A14	1.00											
A15	0.66[a]	1.00										
A16	0.46[a]	0.47[a]	1.00									
A17	0.64[a]	0.75[a]	0.40[a]	1.00								
A18	0.58[a]	0.83[a]	0.42[a]	0.75[a]	1.00							
A19	0.45[a]	0.41[a]	0.22	0.36[a]	0.41[a]	1.00						
A20	0.41[a]	0.59[a]	0.22	0.46[a]	0.64[a]	0.34[a]	1.00					
A21	0.44[a]	0.66[a]	0.33[a]	0.50[a]	0.64[a]	0.42[a]	0.79[a]	1.00				
A22	0.09	0.07	0.16	0.00	0.30	0.43[a]	0.09	0.29[a]	1.00			
A23	0.17	0.43[a]	0.09	0.27[a]	0.44[a]	0.39[a]	0.44[a]	0.66[a]	0.56[a]	1.00		
A24	0.41[a]	0.64[a]	0.27[a]	0.40[a]	0.61[a]	0.36[a]	0.74[a]	0.87[a]	0.38[a]	0.73[a]	1.00	
A25	0.41[a]	0.45[a]	0.45[a]	0.41[a]	0.40[a]	0.21	0.20	0.25[a]	0.19	0.17	0.35[a]	1.00

[a]Significant at the .05 level or less.

Table 4-3
Current Effective Standards of Regulation for Each
Depository Intermediary

Regulation	Commercial Bank	Mutual Savings Bank	S&L	Credit Union
β	0.072	0.018	0.020	0.00
$\bar{R}_D$	1.21%	1.30%	1.32%	1.35%
σ_{R_D}	0.154%	0.096%	0.135%	0.085%
ρ	0.56	0.62	0.68	0.88

The results of these calculations are presented in table 4-3.

2. To estimate the important parameters of the cost of funds, the effective total cost of funds was first calculated for each period.[14] Specifically, total interest expense plus operating expense less any service charges and fees was divided by total deposits.[15] These data were then used to calculate the average cost of funds $\bar{R}_D$ and the variance of the cost of funds $\sigma_{R_D}^2$. The correlation between the average cost of funds and the return on total available funds was then estimated. The results of these calculations are presented in table 4-3.

3. The effective restrictions placed on the capitalization of each type of depository institution do appear to be the same order of magnitude. Indeed, over the period 1969-1977 the industry average capital-asset ratio for each type of intermediary was approximately 5.5 percent. As an upper bound, we assume the effective leverage constraint L_{max} to be 19 for all types of firms.

Notes

1. Note that solvency regulation not only affects the profitability and risk of an intermediary but also its probability of insolvency (see chapter 6).

2. See *Commission on Financial Structure and Regulation, Report of the Commission* (Washington, D.C.: Government Printing Office, 1971), better known as the "Hunt Commission Report." Changes in deposit-rate ceilings and reserve requirements have more recently been proposed by the Federal Reserve Board. See P. Battey, "Fed Draft Offers Reserve Interest, Service Fees, Eased Requirements for Demand Deposits," *American Banker* (June 1978), p. 1, for a discussion of particular aspects of this proposal.

3. The tests for normality (see table 4-1) were not altogether conclusive, but the assumption of normality does not appear unreasonable. It is important to recognize that a large portion of each return is determined by interest/dividend payments and changes in capital values; losses contribute little to the sample rates of return given the extremely small loss rates experienced in these assets. Therefore, even though the distribution of losses is clearly not normal, it

is not unreasonable for capital changes and interest payments' rates of return to be so distributed. Therefore, it is not unreasonable for the underlying distributions of rates of return to be normal.

4. For a complete discussion of the Studentized Range Test, see M.G. Kendall and A. Stuart, *The Advanced Theory of Statistics*, Vol. 2 (New York: Hafner Publishing, 1961), pp. 527-530. The Studentized Range Test statistic is defined as the maximum observed value in the sample minus the minimum observed value in the sample divided by the sample standard deviation.

5. Yields to maturity for 3.5-year and 7.5-year U.S. government bonds as well as all corporate and municipal bonds (for 1-, 10-, and 20-year maturities) are published on a quarterly basis by both Standard and Poor's, Inc., and Moody's Corporation. Given the maturity date, coupon rate, and the yield to maturity, the price of the bond is determined. Thus

$$R_t^N \cong \frac{(F - P_t)/N + iF}{(P_t + F)/2} \quad : \text{an approximation of yield to maturity}$$

where

R_t^N = yield to maturity.

F = face value of bond.

i = coupon rate.

N = number of periods to maturity.

P_t = price of bond at the beginning of time period t.

The yields on six- and twelve-month U.S. government discount bills are quoted on a bank discount-rate basis. The discount basis quotation can be converted to a price in the following manner

$$C = \frac{A}{360} B$$

$$P = 100 - C$$

where

A = days to maturity (days held).

B = discount basis.

C = full discount.

P = dollar price.

See The First Boston Corporation, *Handbook of Securities of the U.S. Government and Federal Agencies* (New York: The First Boston Corporation, 1976),
pp. 56-59, for application of these formulas.

6. Acquisition and service costs for each type of investment category were
estimated using the data presented in *Functional Cost Analysis* (1969-1977).
Acquisition costs were estimated in terms of per dollar of investment. Expected
dollar default per dollar of investment was also estimated from data reported in
Functional Cost Analysis (1969-1977). However, because these data are reported
on an annual basis, as opposed to a quarterly basis, quarterly loan losses per
dollar of investment had to be estimated. Using the annual data, the default rate
for each type of amortized loan category (that is, mortgages, automobile loans,
personal loans, mobile home loans, and other consumer loans, and commercial
loans) was regressed on either the unemployment rate or the gross national
product. Presumably, loss rates are a function of either of these two independent
variables. Quarterly loan-default rates were then estimated using these regression
equations (see appendix B, which reports the results of these regressions). It is
important to note that we implicitly assume that the loss experience of each
type of intermediary does not differ. In the long run this does not appear to be
unreasonable.

7. No attempt was made to detrend the raw data. Certainly, if interest
rates were systematically rising during the period 1969-1977, then our estimates
of the expected rate of return and standard deviation of returns would be under
and overestimated, respectively. However, interest rates rose slowly from 1969
to 1974, peaked, and then fell from 1975 to 1977. Therefore, our estimates are
not systematically biased.

8. The focus of chapter 5 is not to predict intermediary behavior but
rather to examine the impact of regulation on the investment frontier and the
profitability of the firm. Nonetheless, an adequate number of sample points
must be collected to provide a reasonable estimate of the rate of return
distribution for each asset category and to estimate the sample ex-ante efficient
frontier. See R.C. Burgess and K.H. Johnson, "The Effects of Sampling
Fluctuations on the Required Impacts of Security Analysis," *Journal of
Financial and Quantitative Analysis* 11 (1976):847-854. They found that a
minimum of 30 historical observations were required to yield efficient portfolio
performance characteristics when the portfolio time horizon is one quarter.

9. The annual percentage rate would be applicable only when the length
of the portfolio horizon is equal to the maturity of the loan. Otherwise, changes
in loan rates would translate into a change in the "market" value of the loan
which in turn changes the rate of return on the loan.

10. For a single-period portfolio analysis, a simple arithmetic average of
historical returns should be used to estimate the expected performance over a
single period. A single-period analysis is based on the probability of drawing a
single outcome out of a random-variable distribution. On the other hand, a
geometric mean is applicable when comparing the ex-post investment perfor-

mance of two or more investment options over several periods. See M.C. Sarnat, "Capital Market Imperfections and the Composition of Optimal Portfolios," *Journal of Finance* 29 (1974):1241-1253.

11. The correlation between i and j is defined as the covariance of i and j divided by the standard deviation of i and the standard deviation of j.

12. Recall from chapter 2 that member S&Ls are not generally subject to sterile reserve requirements. However, the majority of S&Ls do hold cash to satisfy their short-term liquidity requirements. Therefore, the figure provided in table 4-3 appears reasonable.

13. The underlying data for these calculations were taken from various issues of *Functional Cost Analysis; National Fact Book of Mutual Savings Banks* (Washington, D.C.: National Association of Mutual Savings Banks); *Savings and Loan Fact Book* (Chicago: U.S. League of Savings Associations); *Report of the National Credit Union Administration* (Washington, D.C.: National Credit Union Administration); *Assets and Liabilities of Commercial Banks and Mutual Savings Bank* (Washington, D.C.: Federal Deposit Insurance Corporation); and *FSLIC-insured Savings and Loan Associations Combined Financial Statements* (Washington, D.C.: Federal Home Loan Bank Board).

14. Data sources are listed in note 13.

15. Data on the maturity mix of deposits and their respective interest rates are not readily available. Therefore, we estimated the cost of total deposits, R_D.

5 Impact of Solvency Regulation: Empirical Findings

This chapter estimates the investment frontiers and risk-return loci of each type of intermediary under several regulatory regimes. These estimates will provide the information necessary to measure the absolute effects of regulation and the relative effects across types of depository institutions. The findings reported here should, however, be viewed as approximations to the actual effects of solvency regulation. This follows for several reasons: (1) The analysis does not formally treat the structure and competitive conditions of each market in which each type of intermediary chooses (or is required) to operate. Surely the competitive conditions of a market will have an important influence on a firm's performance and risk and, therefore, on its risk-return locus. Nevertheless, on balance these factors will affect all institutions in the same way; accordingly, the abstraction will not necessarily bias the results systematically. (2) An index is used to represent each investment or asset category. Therefore, the degree of diversification that may be achieved within each investment category cannot be adequately represented. Accordingly, intermediaries that face a very limited investment opportunity set (for example, S&Ls) may appear more severely affected by portfolio restrictions than may actually be the case. Nonetheless, the analysis will still shed light on the broad and relative effects of portfolio restrictions. (3) The analysis is conducted on a pretax basis. As we discussed in chapter 2, each type of intermediary is subject to a different tax structure. For example, credit unions do not pay any federal taxes. In contrast, the income of commercial banks, S&Ls, and mutual banks is subject to federal taxation. Further, each type of intermediary is permitted to place a certain amount of income into loss and contingency reserves, which reduces the effective tax rate. Undoubtedly the tax structure will influence the particular portfolio selected by an intermediary. However, a posttax analysis would require a thorough examination of these various tax structures to ensure that the results are not biased in an unknown and subtle way. For simplicity, the analysis is carried out on a pretax basis. (4) The portfolio horizon for each intermediary is assumed to be one quarter of a year. Prices of assets with maturities closest to this portfolio horizon will fluctuate less with changes in interest rates than the prices of assets with longer maturities. Therefore, intermediaries that specialize in short-term assets may appear to hold a less risky portfolio. Consequently, because of the portfolio horizon assumed in this analysis, our results may systematically underestimate the effects of regulations on credit unions and commercial banks (since both are permitted to invest extensively in short-term loans) and overestimate these effects on thrift institutions given the current make-up of their portfolios.

The empirical investigation proceeds as follows. First, the effects of asset restrictions on the investment frontier are investigated. To conduct this analysis, we use a quadratic programming algorithm to generate the efficient frontiers under various asset restrictions. These frontiers are then compared to the unconstrained frontier. Second, the risk-return locus (that is, equation 3.17) of each type of intermediary is presented. Recall that the derivation of this locus is based on the assumptions that an intermediary borrows at the risk-free rate R_o and that no reserve requirements exist. This analysis will yield a risk-ratio for each intermediary that can be compared to the unconstrained regime (see figure 3-4). Third, Regulation Q rate ceilings and leverage constraints are introduced, and the efficient risk-return boundary (or locus) of each intermediary is examined. Finally, the sensitivity of each risk-return boundary to changes in the principal solvency standards is reported.

Effects of Asset Restrictions on the Investment Frontier

An efficient portfolio is characterized by the allocation of funds X_i that minimize the risk (variance) of the portfolio for a given target rate of return. Changing the target rate of return on the portfolio requires that a new allocation be found that minimizes its risk. The optimal allocation of total available funds (X_i) can be found with a quadratic programming algorithm.[1] Iterating through this procedure over a number of different expected or target rates of return leads to the efficient frontier.

Introducing the appropriate exclusion and quantity constraints into the universe of financial assets will define the investment opportunity set for each intermediary under the current regulatory regime. Applying the quadratic solution technique to each of these sets over a range of target returns will yield the respective efficient frontiers. For simplicity of comparison, the expected pretax net operating rate of return varies from 1.80 percent to 2.20 percent per quarter, inclusively. The investment frontier will of course extend beyond a target rate of return of 2.20 percent for those intermediaries that are permitted to purchase assets that yield an expected rate of return that is greater than 2.20 percent (for example, the industrial equity index yields an expected rate of return of 2.75 percent).[2] However, this segment of the efficient frontier (incremented by 0.05 percent) will provide adequate information to measure the relative effects of asset restrictions.

Tables 5-1 through 5-4 report the characteristics of each type of intermediary's efficient investment frontier under the current regulatory regime.[3] Column 1 of each table indicates which assets are excluded from consideration by regulation.[4]

Table 5-1
Current Regulatory Regime, Commercial Bank Investment Frontier A
(Percentage Composition of Efficient Portfolios)

	1	2	3	4	5	6	7	8	9
A1	–	–	–	–	–	–	–		
A2	–	–	–	–	–	–	–		
A3	–	–	–	–	–	–	–		
A4	–	–	–	–	–	–	–		
A5	3.1	–	–	–	–	–	–		
A6	–	0.6	1.4	–	–	–	–		
A7	70.3	77.9	83.7	–	–	–	–		
A8	–	–	–	–	–	–	–		
A9	5.9	1.6	–	–	–	–	–		
A10	7.8	9.4	12.1	95.0	70.0	45.0	20.0		
A11	1.0	1.1	0.9	–	–	–	–		
A12	–	–	–	–	–	–	–	Infeasible	
A13	6.3	4.1	–	–	–	–	–		
A14	0.8	1.2	1.4	–	–	–	–		
A15*	–	–	–	–	–	–	–		
A16*	–	–	–	–	–	–	–		
A17*	–	–	–	–	–	–	–		
A18*	–	–	–	–	–	–	–		
A19	4.6	4.1	–	–	–	–	–		
A20	–	–	0.5	5.0	30.0	55.0	80.0		
A21*	–	–	–	–	–	–	–		
A22*	–	–	–	–	–	–	–		
A23*	–	–	–	–	–	–	–		
A24*	–	–	–	–	–	–	–		
A25*	–	–	–	–	–	–	–		
Portfolio return (%)	1.80	1.85	1.90	1.95	2.00	2.05	2.10		
Standard deviation (%)	0.14	0.14	0.15	0.38	1.36	2.51	3.70		
Shadow price	0.02	0.03	0.10	3.33	30.80	58.18	85.61		

*Indicates assets excluded from the investment opportunity set.

As the tables indicate, the investment opportunity sets of commercial banks and credit unions yield far superior investment frontiers relative to those of mutual savings banks and S&Ls. For example, an expected rate of return of 1.80 percent implies a portfolio risk (standard deviation) of 0.14 percent and 0.13 percent for commercial banks and credit unions, respectively. For the same target return, however, mutual savings banks and S&Ls must assume a significantly larger portfolio risk of 1.34 percent and 3.47 percent, respectively.[5]

The efficient frontier of a commercial bank extends to a maximum rate of return of 2.10 percent. This implies that no asset is permitted in a commercial bank's opportunity set that offers an expected rate of return that is greater than this amount. In contrast, a mutual savings bank has an efficient frontier that extends way beyond 2.20 percent since equity investments are permitted in its investment set. Note the commercial bank frontier and mutual bank frontier cross at approximately 2.10 percent.

The risk-return characteristics of an S&L's portfolio appears to be influenced dramatically by the mortgage constraint. For a target rate of return of

Table 5-2
Current Regulatory Regime, Mutual Savings Bank Investment Frontier A
(Percentage Composition of Efficient Portfolios)

	1	2	3	4	5	6	7	8	9
A1	—	—	—	—	—	—	—	—	—
A2	81.7	75.5	68.7	61.8	55.0	48.2	41.4	34.5	27.7
A3	—	—	—	—	—	—	—	—	—
A4	—	—	—	—	—	—	—	—	—
A5*	—	—	—	—	—	—	—	—	—
A6*	—	—	—	—	—	—	—	—	—
A7*	—	—	—	—	—	—	—	—	—
A8*	—	—	—	—	—	—	—	—	—
A9*	—	—	—	—	—	—	—	—	—
A10*	—	—	—	—	—	—	—	—	—
A11	—	—	—	—	—	—	—	—	—
A12	1.2	—	—	—	—	—	—	—	—
A13	—	—	—	—	—	—	—	—	—
A14	—	—	—	—	—	—	—	—	—
A15	—	—	—	—	—	—	—	—	—
A16*	—	—	—	—	—	—	—	—	—
A17*	—	—	—	—	—	—	—	—	—
A18*	—	—	—	—	—	—	—	—	—
A19	—	—	—	—	—	—	—	—	—
A20	8.1	12.6	16.6	20.6	24.6	28.6	32.6	36.6	40.7
A21	—	—	—	—	—	—	—	—	—
A22*	—	—	—	—	—	—	—	—	—
A23*	—	—	—	—	—	—	—	—	—
A24*	—	—	—	—	—	—	—	—	—
A25	8.1	11.8	14.7	17.5	20.4	23.2	26.0	28.8	31.6
Portfolio return (%)	1.80	1.85	1.90	1.95	2.00	2.05	2.10	2.15	2.20
Standard deviation (%)	1.34	1.57	1.83	2.11	2.40	2.70	2.98	3.28	3.58
Shadow price	6.00	7.80	9.81	11.81	13.80	15.80	17.80	19.80	21.79

*Indicates assets excluded from the investment opportunity set.

1.80 percent, S&Ls must assume a portfolio risk of 3.47 percent. This is significantly greater than the portfolio risk assumed by the other intermediaries for an identical portfolio return. In addition, the mortgage constraint limits an S&L's frontier to a maximum target rate of return of only 1.90 percent with a corresponding risk of 4.43 percent. In comparison, a credit union's frontier, while also limited to a maximum target return of 1.90 percent, implies a risk of only 0.16 percent. Accordingly, credit unions, though limited by portfolio restrictions, are significantly less risky than S&Ls. (See figure 5-1, which illustrates the investment frontier of each intermediary.)

To put these investment frontiers in perspective, table 5-5 presents the characteristics of the unconstrained efficient frontier. As we might expect, the unconstrained investment frontier dominates the constrained frontier of each intermediary. While the frontiers of both commercial banks and credit unions do

Table 5-3
Current Regulatory Regime, S&L Investment Frontier A
(Percentage Composition of Efficient Portfolios)

	1	2	3	4	5	6	7	8	9
A1	—	—	—						
A2	—	—	—						
A3	—	—	—						
A4	—	—	—						
A5*	—	—	—						
A6*	—	—	—						
A7	—	—	—						
A8	—	—	—						
A9*	—	—	—						
A10	—	—	—						
A11	32.2	18.3	4.4			Infeasible			
A12	47.8	61.7	75.6						
A13	—	—	—						
A14	—	—	—						
A15	—	—	—						
A16*	—	—	—						
A17*	—	—	—						
A18*	—	—	—						
A19	—	—	—						
A20	20.0	20.0	20.0						
A21	—	—	—						
A22*	—	—	—						
A23*	—	—	—						
A24*	—	—	—						
A25*	—	—	—						
Portfolio return (%)	1.80	1.85	1.90						
Standard deviation (%)	3.47	3.92	4.43						
Shadow price	29.71	37.94	46.17						

*Indicates assets excluded from the investment opportunity set.

not differ significantly from the unconstrained frontier for expected rates of return of 1.90 percent or less, the unconstrained investment frontier clearly dominates in all other cases. Moreover, the unconstrained investment frontier significantly dominates the investment frontiers of both mutual savings banks and S&Ls.

Introducing additional assets into the feasible opportunity set will result in a more favorable investment frontier for each intermediary. Tables 5-6 through 5-9 report the characteristics of each intermediary's efficient frontier after eliminating or relaxing the major asset restrictions.[6] Thus commercial bank investment frontier D is the unconstrained frontier with equity excluded. Mutual savings bank frontier C is derived from an opportunity set containing all assets but Baa bonds. The S&L frontier C' was derived after all asset restrictions were eliminated and the mortgage constraint changed from 80 percent to 40 percent.

Table 5-4
Current Regulatory Regime, Credit Union Investment Frontier A
(Percentage Composition of Efficient Portfolios)

	1	2	3	4	5	6	7	8	9
A1	1.2	–	–						
A2	–	–	–						
A3	–	–	–						
A4	–	0.1	0.7						
A5*	–	–	–						
A6*	–	–	–						
A7	69.8	79.8	89.5						
A8*	–	–	–						
A9	12.7	5.1	–						
A10	8.6	8.6	7.9						
A11*	–	–	–						
A12*	–	–	–			Infeasible			
A13	6.2	4.5	0.3						
A14	1.5	1.8	1.6						
A15*	–	–	–						
A16*	–	–	–						
A17*	–	–	–						
A18*	–	–	–						
A19*	–	–	–						
A20*	–	–	–						
A21*	–	–	–						
A22*	–	–	–						
A23*	–	–	–						
A24*	–	–	–						
A25*	–	–	–						
Portfolio return (%)	1.80	1.85	1.90						
Standard deviation (%)	0.13	0.14	0.16						
Shadow price	0.01	0.03	0.09						

*Indicates assets excluded from the investment opportunity set.

Finally, all assets have been introduced into the opportunity set of a credit union (other than municipals) to derive the credit union frontier E.[7]

As we might expect, the efficient frontier of each intermediary improves significantly after a change in portfolio restrictions. The intermediaries that gain the most from this change in regulation are mutual savings banks and S&Ls. Comparison of the mutual savings banks' efficient frontier before and after the change in asset restrictions reveals that the risk per unit of return decreases substantially. For example, prior to the change in asset restrictions, a mutual savings bank assumed a 1.34 percent portfolio risk for 1.80 percent expected return on its portfolio. In contrast, after the change in asset restrictions, portfolio risk is only 0.12 percent. Savings and loans are similarly affected. Thus an expected rate of return of 1.80 percent now implies a portfolio risk of only 1.16 percent as opposed to 3.47 percent prior to the change in asset restrictions and the mortgage constraint.[8]

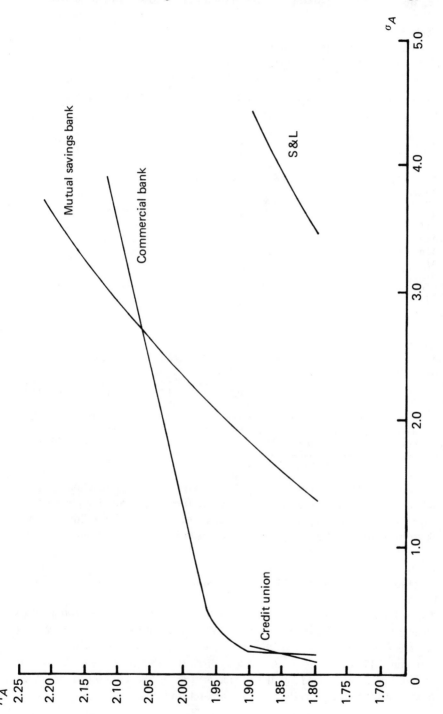

Figure 5-1. Efficient Frontier of Each Intermediary under the Current Regulatory Regime

Table 5-5
Unconstrained Investment Frontier
(Percentage Composition of Efficient Portfolios)

	1	2	3	4	5	6	7	8	9
A1	–	–	–	–	–	–	–	–	–
A2	–	–	–	–	–	–	–	–	–
A3	–	–	–	–	–	–	–	–	–
A4	–	–	–	–	–	–	–	–	–
A5	7.2	5.5	1.1	–	–	–	–	–	–
A6	–	–	–	–	–	–	–	–	–
A7	60.8	68.2	75.5	35.1	–	–	–	–	–
A8	–	–	–	–	–	–	–	–	–
A9	7.3	2.6	–	–	–	–	–	–	–
A10	7.4	7.4	7.4	39.7	77.8	83.2	75.4	67.7	59.9
A11	0.9	0.9	0.6	–	–	–	–	–	–
A12	–	–	–	–	–	–	–	–	–
A13	4.2	2.5	1.8	–	–	–	–	–	–
A14	–	–	–	–	–	–	–	–	–
A15	–	–	–	–	–	–	–	–	–
A16	2.7	1.7	–	–	–	–	–	–	–
A17	–	–	–	–	–	–	–	–	–
A18	0.4	0.6	0.8	–	–	–	–	–	–
A19	0.6	–	–	–	–	–	–	–	–
A20	–	–	–	1.0	–	–	–	–	–
A21	–	–	–	–	–	–	–	–	–
A22	8.5	10.7	12.7	22.4	13.6	–	–	–	–
A23	–	–	–	–	–	–	–	–	–
A24	–	–	–	0.1	3.8	8.9	11.9	15.8	19.7
A25	–	–	0.2	1.7	4.8	8.8	12.7	16.6	20.5
Portfolio return (%)	1.80	1.85	1.90	1.95	2.00	2.05	2.10	2.15	2.20
Standard deviation (%)	0.11	0.11	0.12	0.22	0.50	0.91	1.35	1.80	2.26
Shadow price	0.00	0.02	0.90	0.90	3.76	7.86	12.10	16.40	20.60

The results presented here clearly indicate that asset restrictions increase rather than decrease the portfolio risk of the firm. Regulators therefore appear to be moving away from their objective of ensuring the solidity of the depository intermediary industry whenever asset restrictions are imposed.

Asset Restrictions and the Risk-Return Locus

The risk-return locus summarizes the opportunities for invested capital. If we assume that an intermediary can raise all its deposits at the risk-free rate R_o and no reserve requirements exist, then the opportunity locus can be represented by equation 3.17. Recall from our previous discussion that the slope of the locus is in large part determined by the characteristics of the asset portfolio. Asset restrictions therefore directly affect the risk-return locus.

Table 5-6
Commercial Bank Investment Frontier D
(Percentage Composition of Efficient Portfolios)

	1	2	3	4	5	6	7	8	9
A1	–	–	–	–	–	–	–	–	–
A2	–	–	–	–	–	–	–	–	–
A3	–	–	–	–	–	–	–	–	–
A4	–	–	–	–	–	–	–	–	–
A5	7.7	5.1	0.9	–	–	–	–	–	–
A6	–	–	–	–	–	–	–	–	–
A7	61.3	68.4	75.5	19.8	–	–	–	–	–
A8	–	–	–	–	–	–	–	–	–
A9	6.9	1.4	–	–	–	–	–	–	–
A10	6.9	8.0	6.9	44.4	57.1	54.2	51.3	48.4	45.8
A11	1.0	1.0	0.8	–	–	–	–	–	–
A12	–	–	–	–	–	–	–	–	–
A13	3.7	2.1	1.4	–	–	–	–	–	–
A14	–	–	–	–	–	–	–	–	–
A15	–	–	–	–	–	–	–	–	–
A16	2.8	1.5	0.2	–	–	–	–	–	–
A17	–	–	–	–	–	–	–	–	–
A18	0.4	0.7	0.8	–	–	–	–	–	–
A19	1.0	–	–	–	–	–	–	–	–
A20	–	–	–	–	–	–	–	–	–
A21	–	–	–	–	–	–	–	–	–
A22	8.3	11.7	13.5	33.5	31.8	23.9	16.9	8.2	–
A23	–	–	–	–	–	–	–	–	–
A24	–	–	–	1.7	11.2	21.9	32.7	43.4	54.2
A25*	–	–	–	–	–	–	–	–	–
Portfolio return (%)	1.80	1.85	1.90	1.95	2.00	2.05	2.10	2.15	2.20
Standard deviation (%)	0.11	0.12	0.13	0.26	0.70	1.27	1.87	2.47	3.10
Shadow price	0.00	0.02	0.04	1.45	7.74	15.10	22.44	29.80	37.14

*Indicates assets excluded from the investment opportunity set.

The effects of asset restrictions can be summarized in terms of the slope of the opportunity locus or the line extending from the risk-free borrowing rate to the tangency point on the risky efficient frontier. We will refer to this slope as the *risk ratio*.[9]

Table 5-10 reports the risk ratios for each intermediary and the risk ratio that results from the unconstrained portfolio. These rates were calculated for three different risk-free borrowing rates. As the table indicates, the risk-return loci of credit unions dominate the loci of other intermediaries for risk-free borrowing rates of 1.15 percent and 1.25 percent. For a risk-free borrowing rate of 1.44 percent, commercial banks dominate all other intermediaries. Nonetheless, the opportunity locus of each intermediary is dominated by the unconstrained locus for any risk-free borrowing rate. Asset restrictions therefore expose the capital of each intermediary to higher risk relative to the unconstrained regime.

Table 5-7
Mutual Savings Bank Investment Frontier C
(Percentage Composition of Efficient Portfolios)

	1	2	3	4	5	6	7	8	9
A2	–	–	–	–					
A3	–	–	–	–					
A4	–	–	–	–					
A5	–	–	–	–					
A6	–	–	0.7	–					
A7	64.2	76.9	82.2	41.8					
A8	–	–	–	–					
A9	11.8	1.0	–	–					
A10	13.2	10.5	13.3	54.3					
A11	0.5	0.5	0.8	–		Same as			
A12	–	–	–	–		Portfolio B			
A13	7.0	6.3	0.6	–	(See appendix D)				
A14	0.9	0.9	0.8	–					
A15	–	–	0.8	–					
A16*	–	–	–	–					
A17*	–	–	–	–					
A18*	–	–	–	–					
A19	2.2	3.3	–	–					
A20	–	–	–	1.5					
A21	–	–	0.1	–					
A22*	–	–	–	–					
A23*	–	–	–	–					
A24*	–	–	–	–					
A25	–	0.3	0.3	2.4					
Portfolio return (%)	1.80	1.85	1.90	1.95					
Standard deviation (%)	0.12	0.13	0.15	0.24					
Shadow price	0.03	0.06	0.07	1.08					

*Indicates assets excluded from the investment opportunity set.

We demonstrated in chapter 3 that reserve requirements reduce the returns to capital per unit of risk. Reserve requirements combined with asset restrictions therefore further reduce the locus of an intermediary in risk-return space (see equation 3.18). For example, the risk ratio of a commercial bank at a borrowing rate of 1.44 percent falls by 25 percent when a 7.2 percent reserve requirement is imposed.[10] Since each type of intermediary (other than credit unions) must satisfy some reserve requirement, the risk ratios presented in table 5-10 actually understate the effect portfolio restrictions have on the risk-return loci. The unconstrained regime therefore implies significantly less risk exposure at any level of return to the portfolio relative to the current regulatory regime.

The analysis presented in this section assumed that deposit-rate ceilings did not exist and that an intermediary could raise all its deposits at a risk-free borrowing rate. These assumptions were made so that we could isolate the effects of portfolio restrictions. We now turn to an empirical analysis of the

Table 5-8
S&L Investment Frontier C′
(Percentage Composition of Efficient Portfolios)

	1	2	3	4	5	6	7	8	9
A1	–	–	–	–	–	–	–	–	–
A2	–	–	–	–	–	–	–	–	–
A3	–	–	–	–	–	–	–	–	–
A4	–	–	–	–	–	–	–	–	–
A5	–	–	–	–	–	–	–	–	–
A6	–	–	–	–	–	–	–	–	–
A7	–	–	–	–	–	–	–	–	–
A8	–	–	–	–	–	–	–	–	–
A9	–	–	–	–	–	–	–	–	–
A10	56.9	30.7	–	–	–	–	–	–	–
A11	34.1	26.2	19.7	16.1	12.2	8.5	4.7	1.0	–
A12	5.9	13.8	20.2	23.9	27.8	31.5	35.3	39.0	40.0
A13	–	–	–	–	–	–	–	–	–
A14	–	–	–	–	–	–	–	–	–
A15	–	–	–	–	–	–	–	–	–
A16	–	–	–	–	–	–	–	–	–
A17	–	–	–	–	–	–	–	–	–
A18	–	–	–	–	–	–	–	–	–
A19	–	–	–	–	–	–	–	–	–
A20	–	–	–	–	–	–	–	–	–
A21	–	–	–	–	–	–	–	–	–
A22	–	22.6	50.9	45.3	39.9	34.4	29.0	23.5	16.2
A23	–	–	–	–	–	–	–	–	–
A24	3.1	6.6	6.4	8.5	10.5	12.5	14.6	16.5	20.1
A25	–	–	2.8	6.2	9.6	13.0	16.5	19.9	23.7
Portfolio return (%)	1.80	1.85	1.90	1.95	2.00	2.05	2.10	2.15	2.20
Standard deviation (%)	1.16	1.37	1.72	2.10	2.48	2.88	3.29	3.70	4.11
Shadow price	3.53	7.42	12.40	16.01	19.61	23.23	26.84	30.45	34.43

risk-return characteristics of the firm subsequent to the introduction of Regulation Q ceilings and leverage constraints.

Deposit-Rate Ceilings, Leverage Constraints, and the Risk-Return Locus

In this section we examine the efficient risk-return locus of each type of intermediary when portfolio restrictions, deposit-rate ceilings, and leverage constraints are operating simultaneously.[11,12] Recall from chapter 3 that the characteristics of the risk-return locus (as described in equation 3.29) are in large part determined by the standards of regulation. Therefore, we can measure the effects of regulation by comparing these characteristics across each intermediary and to the unconstrained regime.

Table 5-9
Credit Union Investment Frontier E
(Percentage Composition of Efficient Portfolios)

	1	2	3	4	5	6	7	8	9
A1	5.4	–	–	–	–				
A2	–	–	–	–	–				
A3	–	–	–	–	–				
A4	–	–	–	–	–				
A5	–	1.6	–	–	–				
A6	–	–	0.3	–	–				
A7	68.4	75.6	84.5	40.1	–				
A8	–	–	–	–	–				
A9	7.5	1.4	–	–	–				
A10	10.2	11.8	11.5	57.2	92.6	.	.	.	.
A11	0.8	0.7	0.3	–	–				
A12	–	–	–	–	–				
A13	6.4	5.4	1.6	–	–				
A14	1.0	0.7	0.7	–	–				
A15	–	–	–	–	–				
A16	–	2.3	–	–	–				
A17	–	–	–	–	–				
A18	–	0.2	0.7	–	–				
A19*	–	–	–	–	–				
A20*	–	–	–	–	–				
A21*	–	–	–	–	–				
A22*	–	–	–	–	–				
A23*	–	–	–	–	–				
A24*	–	–	–	–	–				
A25	–	0.2	0.4	2.7	7.4				
Portfolio return (%)	1.80	1.85	1.90	1.95	2.00				
Standard deviation (%)	0.11	0.11	0.12	0.25	0.25				
Shadow price	0.00	0.02	0.06	0.16	0.16				

*Indicates assets excluded from the investment opportunity set.

Table 5-10
Risk Ratios of Depository Intermediaries for Different Values of the Risk-free Borrowing Rate

Borrowing Rate (R_O)	Risk Ratio				
	Commercial Bank	Mutual Savings Bank	S&L	Credit Union	Unconstrained Regime
1.15	4.78	0.79	0.61	5.03	6.39
1.25	4.18	0.61	0.49	4.34	5.62
1.44	3.15	0.34	0.21	2.87	3.83

Note: The tangent portfolio is taken from efficient frontier A for each intermediary. The risk ratios are based on the assumptions that Regulation Q ceilings and leverage constraints do not exist and that reserves are not required. The unconstrained regime is based on the unconstrained portfolio presented in table 5-5.

Table 5-11 sets out the characteristics of the efficient risk-return locus of each intermediary under the current regulatory regime.[13] These characteristics include the expected return to capital $\bar{R}_K$, the capital-asset ratio $1/1 + L$, and the investment exposure α_R, per unit of risk σ_K. (Note that probability of failure over these loci are presented in chapter 6.) It also reports these same characteristics for an unconstrained intermediary.[14]

As the data in table 5-11 indicate, the risk-return loci of credit unions and commercial banks are far superior to those of mutual savings banks and S&Ls. Over the risk interval 0.25 percent to 1.75 percent, credit unions and commercial banks can expect to earn on their capital 3.45 percent to 11.72 percent and 2.55 percent to 8.68 percent, respectively. In contrast, for the same risk levels mutual savings banks and S&Ls can expect to earn only 1.89 percent to 4.28 percent and 1.69 percent to 3.18 percent on their capital, respectively.

On the one hand, relative to the unconstrained intermediary, only credit unions and commercial banks can provide approximately similar risk-return opportunities for their invested capital. (Note that this would tend to support the empirical observation that credit unions and commercial banks have both grown at faster rates than the other intermediaries.) This is due in large part to the small variance of the cost of funds for credit unions, the low average cost of funds for commercial banks, and the relatively favorable asset restrictions imposed on both types of intermediaries. It would appear therefore that solvency regulation has not unfavorably affected these institutions.[15]

On the other hand, the risk-return locus of the unconstrained intermediary is clearly superior to the loci of the thrift institutions. For example, at $\sigma_K = 1.75$ percent, the unconstrained intermediary can expect to earn 9.26 percent on its capital. This is in contrast to 4.28 percent, and 3.18 percent for mutual savings banks, and S&Ls, respectively. It seems that solvency regulation has unfavorably affected the risk and profitability of these institutions.

A minimum capital-asset ratio is assumed to be 0.05 under the current regulatory regime. This ratio limits the operating area of a credit union; thus the legitimate portion of the risk-return locus is prevented from extending beyond a risk level of 1.75 percent. Commercial banks are similarly affected but to a much lesser degree. Thus the locus of a commercial bank can extend up to and beyond a risk level of 2.75 percent, yet the rate of return drops significantly because of the binding capital-asset ratio. Undoubtedly, a bank will never select any point on its locus that is partially constrained by the leverage restriction since it could do much better by simply moving down to a lower risk level.

The leverage constraint does not appreciably affect either mutual savings banks or S&Ls over the risk interval specified in table 5-11. This is due to the riskiness of their asset portfolios. That is, neither of these intermediaries need to leverage dramatically to produce the levels of risk specified.

On balance, asset restrictions most severely affect the risk-return loci of mutual savings banks and S&Ls. Relative to the unconstrained intermediary, these institutions earn a significantly lower return on capital yet enjoy a lower average cost of funds. These firms are therefore unable to offset the adverse effects of portfolio restrictions with Regulation Q ceilings. In comparison, credit unions pay higher deposit rates than thrift institutions, yet earn superior returns. This can in large part be attributable to their relatively favorable investment opportunity set and the low variance of their cost of funds. It appears that commercial banks are able to completely offset the effects of portfolio restrictions with the lowest average cost of funds of any intermediary. Their risk-return locus is comparable to the locus of the unconstrained intermediary. The current regulatory regime therefore appears to favor credit unions and commercial banks over thrift institutions. (See figure 5-2, which plots the risk-return locus of each intermediary under the current regulatory regime.)

Sensitivity of the Risk-Return Locus to Changes in the Solvency Standards

This section reports the sensitivity of the risk-return characteristics of each depository intermediary to small changes in the solvency standards. Specifically, we examine and compare the change in each risk-return locus when: (1) the acceptable capital-asset ratio falls by 5 percent, (2) reserve requirements increase by 5 percent, (3) Regulation Q ceilings increase by 5 percent, and (4) Regulation Q ceilings increase by 5 percent and asset restrictions are almost entirely eliminated.

   This analysis will indicate which solvency parameters most severely affect each intermediary's risk-return locus. This in turn will provide regulators with at least a feeling for the "orders of magnitude" effects that solvency regulation has on each type of intermediary. Regulators can then more knowledgeably shift the regulatory instruments to achieve their objectives without unfavorably changing the risk-return opportunities of a depository intermediary.

   As the data in table 5-11 indicate, a capital-asset constraint of 0.05 significantly limits the operating area of credit unions and to a lesser extent commercial banks. In comparison, thrift institutions are not noticeably affected by the capital constraint. Accordingly, a 5 percent decrease in the acceptable capital-asset ratio should not meaningfully change the risk-return characteristics of thrift institutions relative to any change that might be exhibited by credit unions and commercial banks.

   A 5-percent decrease in the acceptable capital-asset ratio results in a 2.5-percent increase in the rate of return for credit unions at a risk level of 1.50 percent. However, credit unions are still constrained from moving past a risk level of 1.75 percent. A slight change in the capital-asset ratio therefore does not significantly improve a credit union's risk-return locus. In contrast, commercial banks can now move to a risk level of 2.75 percent without experiencing a sharp drop in earnings. Indeed, at the risk level of 2.75 percent, a 5-percent decrease in

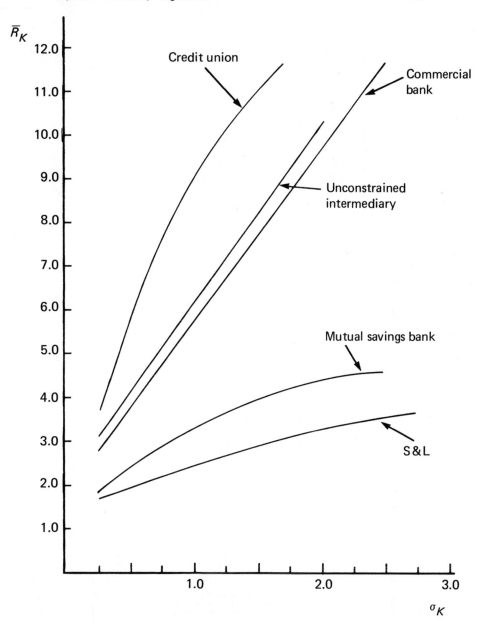

Figure 5-2. Risk-Return Locus of Each Intermediary under the Current Regulatory Regime

the capital-asset ratio yields a 273 percent increase in rate of return. Although there is a large marginal increase in earnings at a risk level of 2.75 percent, the change in the ratio does not permit commercial banks from moving past this risk

Table 5-11
Risk-Return Characteristics of Depository Intermediaries under the Current Regulatory Regime
(Percent)

Risk σ_K	Commercial Bank			Mutual Savings Bank			S&L			Credit Union			Unconstrained Intermediary
	$\bar{R}_K$	$\frac{1}{1+L}$	α_R	$\bar{R}_K$	$\frac{1}{1+L}$	α_R	$\bar{R}_K$	$\frac{1}{1+L}$	α_R	$\bar{R}_K$	$\frac{1}{1+L}$	α_R	$\bar{R}_K$
0.25	2.55	41.66	89.00	1.89	23.25	7.0	1.69	29.41	10.0	3.45	14.50	50.00	3.11
0.50	3.62	23.92	100.00	2.34	13.15	7.0	1.93	16.66	10.0	5.47	8.13	56.61	4.16
0.75	4.65	16.47	100.00	2.78	9.17	7.0	2.19	12.19	13.3	7.50	5.43	56.61	5.20
1.00	5.66	12.66	100.00	3.22	6.99	7.0	2.43	9.4	13.3	9.00	5.13	70.00	6.21
1.25	6.67	10.20	100.00	3.67	6.09	10.0	2.68	7.6	13.3	9.80	5.32	83.25	7.23
1.50	7.68	8.62	100.00	4.12	5.10	10.0	2.93	6.4	13.3	10.68	5.26	93.24	8.25
1.75	8.68	8.06	100.00	4.28	5.15	13.0	3.18	5.5	13.3	11.72	5.02	100.00	9.26
2.00	9.68	7.00	100.00	4.28	5.46	17.0	3.35	5.3	17.0		Infeasible		10.28
2.25	10.68	5.81	100.00	4.24	5.84	20.0	3.42	5.4	20.0				8.73
2.50	11.69	5.26	100.00	4.57	5.29	20.0	3.44	5.6	23.3				7.52
2.75	4.64	5.08	10.00	4.50	5.65	23.0	3.65	5.1	23.3				6.25

Solvency Parameters

	Commercial Bank	Mutual Savings Bank	S&L	Credit Union
β (%)	7.2	1.8	2.0	0.0
$\bar{R}_D$ (%)	1.21	1.30	1.32	1.35
Risky portfolio	A	A	A	A

Note: $L_{max} = 19$.

Table 5-12
Risk-Return Characteristics of Depository Intermediaries after a 5-percent Increase in Required Reserves
(Percent)

Risk σ_K	Commercial Bank			Mutual Savings Bank			S&L			Credit Union		
	$\bar{R}_K$	$\frac{1}{1+L}$	α_R	$\bar{R}_K$	$\frac{1}{1+L}$	α_R	$\bar{R}_K$	$\frac{1}{1+L}$	α_R	$\bar{R}_K$	$\frac{1}{1+L}$	α_R
0.25	2.54	43.48	93.24	1.89	23.81	6.70	1.68	29.41	10.00	3.37	15.15	53.28
0.50	3.60	23.81	100.00	2.33	13.15	6.70	1.92	16.67	10.00	5.31	8.06	56.61
0.75	4.62	16.45	100.00	2.77	9.17	6.70	2.16	12.34	13.32	7.23	5.71	56.61
1.00	5.62	12.66	100.00	3.21	7.04	6.70	2.40	9.43	13.32	8.76	5.05	70.00
1.25	6.61	10.20	100.00	3.65	6.06	10.00	2.65	7.63	13.32	9.61	5.23	83.25
1.50	7.61	8.62	100.00	4.10	5.15	10.00	2.89	6.41	13.32	10.49	5.18	93.24
1.75	8.60	7.41	100.00	4.25	5.15	13.32	3.13	5.52	13.32			
2.00	9.60	6.53	100.00	4.26	5.46	16.65	3.30	5.31	16.65		Infeasible	
2.25	10.58	5.81	100.00	4.22	5.88	20.00	3.37	5.43	20.00			
2.50	11.57	5.26	100.00	4.55	5.29	20.00	3.40	5.65	23.31			
2.75	4.52	5.10	10.00	4.49	5.68	23.31	3.60	5.12	23.31			

Solvency Parameters

	Commercial Bank	Mutual Savings Bank	S&L	Credit Union
β (%)	7.6	1.9	2.1	1.0
$\bar{R}_D$ (%)	1.21	1.30	1.32	1.35
Risky portfolio	A	A	A	A

Note: $L_{max} = 19$.

Table 5-13
Risk-Return Characteristics of Depository Intermediaries after a 5-percent Increase in Deposit-rate Ceilings
(Percent)

Risk	Commercial Bank			Mutual Savings Bank			S&L			Credit Union		
σ_K	$\bar{R}_K$	$\frac{1}{1+L}$	α_R	$\bar{R}_K$	$\frac{1}{1+L}$	α_R	$\bar{R}_K$	$\frac{1}{1+L}$	α_R	$\bar{R}_K$	$\frac{1}{1+L}$	α_R
0.25	2.48	43.48	96.57	1.71	23.25	6.70	1.55	33.33	13.32	3.07	15.15	53.28
0.50	3.47	23.81	100.00	2.00	14.28	10.00	1.65	17.85	13.32	4.71	8.13	56.61
0.75	4.40	16.47	100.00	2.30	9.90	10.00	1.76	13.88	16.65	6.35	5.71	60.00
1.00	5.33	12.66	100.00	2.54	8.13	10.00	1.87	10.42	16.65	7.74	5.13	70.00
1.25	6.25	10.20	100.00	2.82	6.50	10.00	1.98	8.47	16.65	8.61	5.32	83.25
1.50	7.16	8.62	100.00	3.10	5.15	10.00	2.09	7.57	16.65	9.50	5.26	94.24
1.75	8.08	7.41	100.00	3.26	5.46	13.32	2.20	6.10	16.65	10.45	5.02	100.00
2.00	9.00	6.53	100.00	3.33	5.88	16.65	2.30	5.35	16.65		Infeasible	
2.25	9.91	5.81	100.00	3.36	5.29	20.00	2.40	5.43	20.00			
2.50	10.83	5.26	100.00	3.60	5.65	20.00	2.46	5.65	23.31			
2.75	3.74	5.07	10.00	3.60		23.31	2.56	5.15	23.31			

Solvency Parameters

	Commercial Bank	Mutual Savings Bank	S&L	Credit Union
β (%)	7.2	1.8	2.0	0.0
$\bar{R}_D$ (%)	1.258	1.355	1.379	1.417
Risky portfolio	A	A	A	A

Note: $L_{max} = 19$.

Table 5-14
Risk-Return Characteristics of Depository Intermediaries after a 5 percent Increase in Deposit-rate Ceilings, with Parameters Shifted Proportionately
(Percent)

Risk σ_K	Commercial Bank			Mutual Savings Bank			S&L			Credit Union		
	$\bar{R}_K$	$\frac{1}{1+L}$	α_R	$\bar{R}_K$	$\frac{1}{1+L}$	α_R	$\bar{R}_K$	$\frac{1}{1+L}$	α_R	$\bar{R}_K$	$\frac{1}{1+L}$	α_R
0.25	2.47	43.47	93.24	1.71	23.25	6.70	1.54	34.48	13.32	2.85	17.54	53.28
0.50	3.45	24.39	100.00	1.98	12.98	6.70	1.65	18.18	13.32	4.27	9.34	56.61
0.75	4.39	16.55	100.00	2.25	10.00	10.00	1.75	12.50	13.32	5.68	6.58	60.00
1.00	5.32	12.65	100.00	2.53	7.63	10.00	1.85	10.86	16.65	7.07	5.23	63.27
1.25	6.24	10.31	100.00	2.81	6.13	10.00	1.96	8.69	16.65	8.10	5.29	76.59
1.50	7.16	8.62	100.00	3.08	5.15	10.00	2.07	7.29	16.65	9.00	5.23	86.58
1.75	8.08	7.60	100.00	3.22	5.26	13.32	2.17	6.25	16.65	9.83	5.21	96.57
2.00	9.00	6.53	100.00	3.28	5.61	16.65	2.28	5.49	16.65		Infeasible	
2.25	9.12	6.21	100.00	3.31	6.02	20.00	2.36	5.61	20.00			
2.50	10.83	5.26	100.00	3.53	5.40	20.00	2.50	5.07	20.00			
2.75	3.20	5.05	3.33	3.54	5.81	23.30	2.52	5.34	23.31			

Solvency Parameters

	Commercial Bank			Mutual Savings Bank			S&L			Credit Union		
β (%)	7.2			1.8			2.0			0.0		
$\bar{R}_D$ (%)	1.258			1.355			1.379			1.417		
Risky portfolio	A			A			A			A		

Note: $L_{max} = 19$.

Table 5-15
Risk-Return Characteristics of Depository Intermediaries after a 5-percent Increase in Rate Ceilings and a Relaxation of Portfolio Restrictions
(Percent)

Risk σ_K	Commercial Bank			Mutual Savings Bank			S&L			Credit Union		
	$\bar{R}_K$	$\frac{1}{1+L}$	α_R	$\bar{R}_K$	$\frac{1}{1+L}$	α_R	$\bar{R}_K$	$\frac{1}{1+L}$	α_R	$\bar{R}_K$	$\frac{1}{1+L}$	α_R
0.25	2.56	43.47	100.00	2.55	29.41	70.00	1.60	33.33	13.32	3.22	17.54	66.60
0.50	3.57	22.73	100.00	3.66	17.54	83.25	1.76	20.41	16.65	5.00	9.26	70.00
0.75	4.53	15.87	100.00	4.77	12.50	90.00	1.92	13.70	16.65	6.78	6.45	73.26
1.00	5.50	13.88	100.00	5.88	9.43	90.00	2.08	10.42	16.65	8.55	5.05	76.60
1.25	6.44	9.80	100.00	7.00	7.81	93.24	2.24	9.52	20.00	10.00	5.10	93.20
1.50	7.39	8.26	100.00	8.10	6.50	93.24	2.40	7.94	20.00			
1.75	8.34	7.14	100.00	9.21	5.75	96.60	2.56	6.85	20.00		Infeasible	
2.00	9.29	6.29	100.00	10.32	5.02	96.60	2.72	6.02	20.00			
2.25	10.23	5.62	100.00				2.90	5.65	20.00			
2.50	11.18	5.10	100.00		Infeasible		3.02	5.24	23.31			
2.75	3.20	5.05	3.33				3.18	5.02	23.31			

Solvency Parameters

	Commercial Bank	Mutual Savings Bank	S&L	Credit Union
β (%)	7.2	1.8	2.0	0.0
$\bar{R}_D$ (%)	1.258	1.355	1.379	1.417
Risky portfolio	D	C	C'	E

Note: $L_{max} = 19$.

level. The same holds true for thrift institutions. A change in the capital-asset ratio only slightly improves the riskier portion of their loci. For the most part, therefore, the capital-asset ratio is not a binding constraint over the risk interval 0.25 percent to 2.75 percent.

Tables 5-12 through 5-15 report the risk-return characteristics of each intermediary after a change in several regulatory standards. Table 5-12 reports the impact of a 5-percent increase in required reserves. On average, the rate of return on capital for commercial banks falls by approximately 1 percent. The same holds true for S&Ls. On the other hand, mutual savings banks experience essentially no drop in earnings. Finally, credit unions experience a decrease in rate of return of approximately 5 percent on average when sterile reserve requirements increase from 0 to 1.0 percent. Table 5-12 clearly indicates that a change in reserve requirements in either direction does not significantly alter the risk-return characteristics of any intermediary. Accordingly, each locus will not shift dramatically relative to the locus of the unconstrained intermediary when reserve requirements change.

Tables 5-13 and 5-14 report the risk-return characteristics of each intermediary after a 5-percent increase in deposit-rate ceilings. Recall from chapter 3 that raising deposit-rate ceilings may only raise the average cost of funds. Alternatively, lifting Regulation Q ceilings may also lower the variance of the cost of funds and raise the correlation between the cost of funds and the return on the portfolio. Tables 5-13 and 5-14 present these two cases respectively.[16]

Table 5-13 indicates that the locus of each intermediary falls dramatically when the average cost of funds rises by 5 percent. Specifically, at a risk level of 1.75 percent the rate of return falls by 6.8 percent, 23.8 percent, 30.8 percent, and 10.8 percent for commercial banks, mutual savings banks, S&Ls, and credit unions, respectively. Regulation Q ceilings therefore affect the risk-return locus to a much greater extent than reserve requirements. Consequently, raising Regulation Q ceilings by 5 percent and lowering reserve requirements by an equal amount will result in a less favorable risk-return locus.

Although all intermediaries will experience some fall in earnings as deposit-rate ceilings rise, thrift institutions will be most seriously affected. Thus a small increase in rate ceilings may lead to their risk-return loci falling even further below the loci of the other intermediaries and the unconstrained intermediary.

Table 5-14 reports the impact of a 5-percent increase in deposit-rate ceilings when all three parameters shift proportionately in the directions discussed earlier. Although the percentage fall in earnings is not identical to the first case, the fall is still dramatic. For example, at a risk level of 1.75 percent, the returns to capital fall by 9.31 percent, 25.7 percent, 32 percent, and 16 percent for commercial banks, mutual savings banks, S&Ls, and credit unions, respectively. The net effect of raising deposit-rate ceilings is in either case a significant fall of each risk-return locus, both absolutely and relative to the unconstrained intermediary.

The results up to now indicate that asset restrictions and Regulation Q ceilings are the important determinants of the basic shape and position of the risk-return locus. Asset restrictions lower the locus in risk-return space. Regulation Q ceilings appear to raise the locus, thereby offsetting to a certain extent the effects of asset restrictions. Table 5-15 reports the risk-return characteristics of each intermediary when asset restrictions are almost entirely eliminated and deposit-rate ceilings are raised simultaneously by 5 percent.

The commercial bank risk-return locus essentially does not change when this regulatory regime is introduced. This should not be surprising. As indicated earlier, a change in asset restrictions does not significantly improve the risk-return characteristics of a commercial bank's efficient frontier. Further, we found that a 5-percent increase in deposit-rate ceilings does not greatly reduce the returns to capital. Accordingly, the changes in the regulatory parameters merely offset each other with respect to the net effect on the firm.

The same does not hold true for a mutual savings bank. Asset restrictions severely affect the risk-return characteristics of this institution's investment frontier. Therefore, a change in asset restrictions will significantly reduce the portfolio risk of the firm and increase returns to capital. However, a 5-percent increase in deposit-rate ceilings results in a significant decrease in returns to capital. Nonetheless, on balance the net effect of a simultaneous change in asset restrictions and Regulation Q ceilings is a substantial improvement in the risk-return locus. Indeed, mutual savings banks should be willing to trade off higher deposit-rate ceilings for a much broader menu of assets from which to choose.

Savings and loan institutions and credit unions both suffer a decline in earnings under this regulatory regime. For example, at a risk level of 1.75 percent, the returns to capital fall by 19 percent and 15 percent for S&Ls and credit unions, respectively. Recall that S&Ls suffer a dramatic drop in earnings as rate ceilings rise. This decline cannot be offset by the small improvement in the investment frontier as asset restrictions are relaxed. The same holds true for credit unions. The slight improvement in the investment frontier cannot neutralize the rise in their average cost of funds.

Summary

This chapter reported the estimated effects of asset restrictions on the investment frontier of each intermediary. It also presented estimates of the simultaneous effects of portfolio restrictions, leverage constraints, and deposit-rate ceilings on each intermediary's risk-return locus. The data indicate that both commercial banks and credit unions face relatively unconstrained investment frontiers. This is in sharp contrast to mutual savings banks and S&Ls, which are severely burdened by asset restrictions. Indeed, even though these institutions are subject to lower reserve requirements and only slightly higher Regulation Q ceilings than commercial banks, their risk-return loci are clearly inferior. In general, the combination of solvency standards that commercial banks and credit unions are subject to interact to provide both types of institutions with risk-return loci that are comparable to the unconstrained regime.

It is interesting to note that one cannot predict the impact on each intermediary of a small change in a regulatory standard. For instance, a 5-percent increase in deposit-rate ceilings may only slightly alter the return one intermediary may earn, yet it may severely affect another.

Given the results presented in this chapter, it appears that asset restrictions most severely affect the profitability of mutual savings banks and S&Ls. Thus thrift institutions would gain the most from a change in asset restrictions, whereas a decrease in required reserves would only marginally improve their risk-return loci. Credit unions and commercial banks suffer their sharpest decrease in return from a slight increase in Regulation Q ceilings.

The current regulatory regime appears to favor commercial banks and credit unions. To ensure that the thrift institutions will be able to compete successfully with these intermediaries for new capital, it seems that a change in regulation is called for. However, an across-the-board change in one solvency parameter, other factors being equal, may give one intermediary a relative advantage over another. These advantages must therefore be carefully analyzed prior to any change in the current regulatory regime.

Notes

1. A simple quadratic programming problem is defined when the objective function is quadratic (for example, the variance of rate of return) and the constraints are linear. The programming algorithm used in this study is from A. Land and S. Powell, *Fortran Codes for Mathematical Programming: Linear, Quadratic and Discrete* (New York: Wiley, 1973).

2. Examination of the data in chapter 4 will reveal that the efficient frontiers also extend below 1.80 percent.

3. Tables 5-1 and 5-4 indicate the partial-equilibrium nature of the empirical analysis. For example, a commercial bank would minimize the variance of its portfolio at a target return of 1.80 percent by investing approximately 70 percent of its total available funds into consumer loans. Obviously, either the market or the authorities would prevent a firm from constructing this portfolio. Nonetheless, the tables present the optimal allocation of funds given the risk-return parameters of each asset. Accordingly, the results illustrate the best possible portfolio that may be achieved. In one sense, therefore, they underestimate the actual effects of portfolio restrictions.

4. Recall that 80 percent of an S&L's total available funds must be held in mortgages. Accordingly, the proportions X_{11} and X_{12} (A11 and A12) must sum to at least 0.80. The frontier of an S&L is generated subject to this constraint.

We have ignored, however, the quantity constraints that limit the amount of capital that can be exposed to a single asset. Recall that these constraints focus on a single borrower, not on an entire category of assets presented here. Given the aggregate level of data, we of course cannot properly introduce these constraints into the investment set; in either case, however, the results would not differ significantly.

5. The S&L frontier exhibits significantly greater portfolio risk than the frontiers of other intermediaries. This is in large part due to the mortgage constraint. Although an S&L may achieve much greater diversification in mortgages that is indicated in table 5-4, the constraint seems to severely exacerbate the risk of an S&L.

6. The efficient frontiers of each intermediary as asset restrictions are relaxed incrementally are presented in appendix D.

7. Recall that credit unions are not taxed by the federal government. Therefore, credit unions will never hold a tax-free bond since the prices of these bonds are presumably determined by investors with positive marginal tax rates.

8. As indicated earlier, the S&L investment frontier is severely affected by the mortgage constraint. Examination of table 5-5 reveals that mortgages enter only marginally in the unconstrained efficient frontier. Accordingly, an 80 percent or even 40 percent mortgage constraint contributes substantial portfolio risk.

9. In symbols, the risk ratio is $(\overline{R}_A - R_o) \div \sigma_A$. In general, it represents the interest spread the firm can earn on its invested capital per unit of risk exposure.

10. The effective average reserve requirement for commercial banks is 7.2 percent. See table 4-3.

11. Recall that the efficient risk-return locus summarizes the opportunities of invested capital. Clearly, the owners (current and potential) of the firm evaluate the risk-adjusted returns they can expect to earn on their invested capital before deciding to retain or invest their funds in the firm. If this return is inadequate relative to alternative investment opportunities, then capital will not be forthcoming and the firm will decline. Moreover, regulators are concerned with the safety of intermediary capital. Accordingly, they will want to evaluate its risk exposure. Consequently, we will now focus solely on the risk-return locus of the firm, which summarizes the important risk characteristics of the firm.

12. This section, as in chapter 3, will assume that each type of intermediary has only two assets in which it can invest its total available funds. The first asset is a portfolio of risky securities whereas the second asset is a risk-free security. The portfolio of risky securities selected in this analysis is tangent to the line extending from the risk-free rate of return to the constrained efficient frontier. This will yield the most efficient asset locus for each intermediary. As we indicated in chapter 3, this assumption allows us to focus on the iteraction of deposit-rate ceilings, leverage constraints, and portfolio restrictions without complicating the empirical analysis unnecessarily.

13. Each locus is generated assuming that the parameters of the cost of funds are not affected as the scale of each intermediary expands. As indicated in chapter 3, it is more than likely that both the expected cost of funds and the variance of the cost of funds will rise as D^* rises. Accordingly, each locus will level off more rapidly than is indicated in the text as these parameters change.

14. The complete risk-return characteristics of the unconstrained intermediary are presented in appendix C. This risk-return locus is based on the following set of assumptions: (1) There are no reserve requirements although the firm may hold some reserves in nonearning assets. (2) The firm selects its risky portfolio from the unconstrained efficient frontier. The particular portfolio selected is the portfolio that is tangent to the line extending from the risk-free rate of return to the unconstrained efficient frontier. (3) No deposit-rate ceilings exist; therefore, the firm must raise all funds at the market-determined rate R_S. Under these assumptions the data presented in various issues of the *Federal Reserve Bulletin* yield the following estimates for the relevant variables: $\bar{R}_S = 1.47$ percent, $\sigma_S = 0.20$, $\rho = 0.85$, and $L_{max} = 20$. It is interesting to note that the variance of the average cost of funds for the unconstrained intermediary is higher than the variance of the average cost of funds for any of the regulated intermediaries.

15. As we mentioned at the beginning of this chapter, the results reported may actually understate the effects of regulation on commercial banks and credit unions and overstate these effects on the thrift institutions. This bias is largely due to the assumption of a uniform portfolio horizon. If data on the maturity and rate structure of deposits were readily available, we could determine the portfolio horizon of each type of intermediary by finding the horizon that maximized the correlation between the return on the asset portfolio (R_R) and the average cost of funds (R_D). It may well be the case that S&Ls have significantly reduced the risk of their asset portfolios, given the restrictions on the portfolio, by appropriately structuring their deposits. As presented in chapter 4, however, the correlations between portfolio returns and cost of funds for each intermediary do not differ significantly. Thus a uniform portfolio of a quarter of a year does not appear to be entirely unreasonable.

16. Not all deposit liabilities are subject to deposit-rate ceilings. Therefore, a 5-percent increase in Regulation Q ceilings will not generally raise the average cost of funds by 5 percent. Based on their respective mix of deposits, a 5-percent increase in deposit-rate ceilings translates into the following percentage changes in the key parameters for each intermediary:

	Commercial Bank	Mutual Savings Bank	S&L	Credit Union
% increase	4.00	4.25	4.5	5

6

Solvency Regulation and the Probability of Bankruptcy

A principal objective of solvency regulation is to protect the capital of a depository intermediary. To accomplish this objective, regulators try to reduce the risk exposure of the firm; their principal instruments are asset restrictions, reserve requirements, regulation of capital, and deposit-rate ceilings.

An important part of this study is to determine whether the principal instruments of solvency regulation in fact promote the safety of an intermediary and reduce its chance of failure.[1] To carry out this analysis, we must translate the effects of solvency regulation on an intermediary's risk-return locus into its risk of default or probability of failure.

This chapter presents the probability of bankruptcy of an intermediary as a function of its risk-return characteristics and the standards of solvency regulation. Once this measure is derived and discussed, we will then estimate the probability of bankruptcy of each intermediary under the current regulatory regime. Following this, the sensitivity of this probability to changes in solvency regulation will be reported.

Probability of Bankruptcy

Bankruptcy or failure of an intermediary occurs whenever the income and capital of the firm falls short of the interest owed to depositors. That is, failure occurs whenever:

$$C_R(1 - \beta')R_R + (C - C_R)(1 - \beta') R_o + K < DR_D \qquad (6.1)$$

where

C_R = dollar amount of total available funds that is invested in the risky portfolio.

(Note that in a multiperiod setting, bankruptcy occurs whenever the present value of the liabilities exceeds the present value of the income stream.)

Dividing equation 6.2 by C and rearranging yields (using the notation defined in chapter 3),

$$R_N < -(\frac{1}{1 + L}) \qquad (6.2)$$

107

Thus bankruptcy occurs whenever the realized net rate of return on total available funds is less than the negative of the capital-asset ratio.

Because the return on the portfolio of risky assets R_R and the price the intermediary must pay to depositors R_D are both uncertain, the incidence of bankruptcy is uncertain. Bankruptcy is therefore a random variable. Assuming that the mean and variance of its distribution is known, we can use Chebychev's inequality to estimate the upper bound on the probability of bankruptcy.[2]

Combining equation 6.2 and Chebychev's inequality yields the upper bound on the probability of failure P as a function of each solvency parameter:

$$P_r(\tilde{R}_N < b) \leqslant \frac{\sigma_N^2}{(\bar{R}_N - b)^2} = P \qquad (6.3)$$

where[3,4]

$$b = -\left(\frac{1}{1+L}\right)$$

$$\frac{\partial P}{\partial \sigma_N^2} > 0, \qquad \frac{\partial P}{\partial R_N} < 0, \qquad \frac{\partial P}{\partial b} > 0$$

Examination of equation 6.3 indicates that the *maximum* upper bound on the probability of failure is largely determined by the parameters of regulation. Regulation of capital sets the floor on the capital-asset ratio (that is, L_{max}). Regulation Q ceilings in large part determine the cost of funds that intermediaries expect to pay for deposits (that is, $\bar{R}_D$), and portfolio restrictions set the value of β and implicitly σ_R^2 for any given value of $\bar{R}_R$. Consequently, regulators implicitly select an "acceptable" maximum upper bound on the probability of failure when they specify the value of each solvency parameter.[5]

Recall from the discussion in chapter 3 that solvency regulations interact to determine the position, basic shape, and operating area of the efficient risk-return locus. For example, the current set of regulations may fix the operating area and position of the locus to be AB in figure 6-1. Regulators have therefore implicitly selected the maximum upper bound on the probability of failure. Specifically, they have fixed the slope of the iso-probability line P_{max}.[6]

An intermediary may select any point on the locus between A and B on which to operate. Should the firm select point B, then its probability of failure is P_{max}; conversely, should the firm select point C, its probability of failure is less than P_{max}. In any event, regulators virtually selected P_{max} as an "acceptable" probability of failure when they fixed the standards of regulation.

Moreover, as regulators change the standards of each solvency instrument, the maximum upper bound on the probability of failure also changes. For

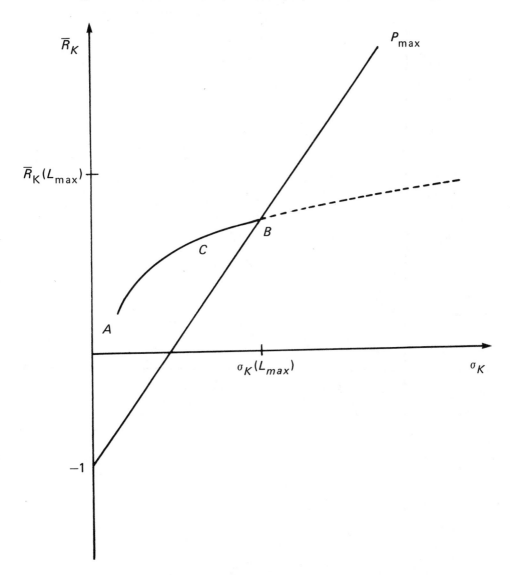

Figure 6-1. Solvency Regulation and the Probability of Bankruptcy

example, say the current set of regulations determine the risk-return locus to be AB in figure 6-2. Assume now that the regulatory authorities eliminate asset restrictions so that the risk-return locus shifts from AB to $A'B'$. Accordingly, the expected rate of return rises for any risk level σ_K. However, the leverage constraint has not been changed, so the permissible operating area of the locus cannot shift past $\sigma_K(L_{max})$. Nonetheless, as figure 6-2 indicates, the maximum

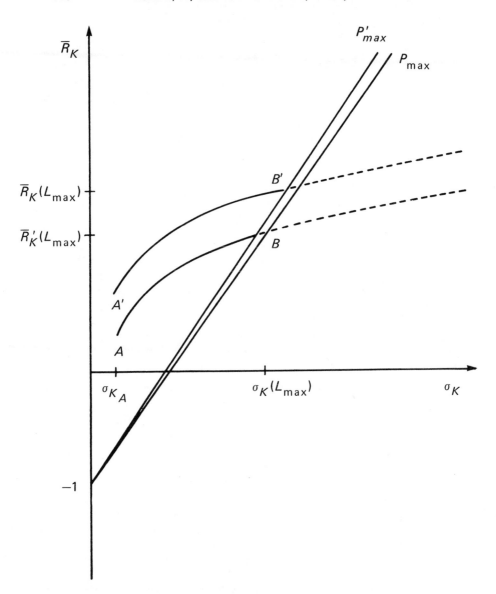

Figure 6-2. Asset Restrictions and the Probability of Bankruptcy

probability of failure falls to P'_{max}. Indeed, for any level of risk between σ_{K_A} and $\sigma_K(L_{max})$, the $A'B'$ locus implies a lower probability of failure. Consequently, the change in regulation has led to a lower maximum probability of failure under the new regulatory regime relative to the earlier regime. However, a lower upper bound was achieved by eliminating the restrictions placed on the portfolio, not by constraining it further.

In general, asset restrictions and reserve requirements increase the probability of bankruptcy in several ways: (1) the firm's risk-return locus falls as these solvency parameters increase, and (2) as profitability declines, the firm may appear less attractive to new investors relative to other investment alternatives, thereby reducing its chance to raise additional capital to support a given level of deposits. This may in turn induce institutions that were previously leveraged below the maximum limit to move towards L_{max}, thus increasing failure exposure.

Deposit-rate ceilings, on the other hand, increase the profitability of an intermediary. These regulations therefore offset to a certain extent the unfavorable effects of portfolio restrictions. Regulation Q ceilings thus appear to function in a desirable fashion as far as failure exposure is concerned. However, recall that deposit-rate ceilings may increase the variance of the cost of funds relative to the unconstrained regime. This in turn will increase σ_K and consequently P. The effect deposit-rate ceilings have on P is therefore ambiguous.

Capital adequacy constraints function in a desirable way in that they constrain an intermediary from operating on the high-risk portion of its locus. However, if the leverage constraint is set too low, the firm may be unable to offset the adverse effects of portfolio restrictions, thereby making it less attractive to new investors relative to an unconstrained firm.

We now turn to estimating the "acceptable" maximum probability of bankruptcy of each intermediary implied by the current regulatory regime. The probability of bankruptcy will also be estimated over the entire risk-return locus for each intermediary. A sensitivity analysis follows.

Probability of Bankruptcy under the
Current Regulatory Regime

As indicated earlier, the maximum probability of failure P_{max} is a function of all regulatory parameters and the risk-return characteristics of an intermediary. Table 6-1 sets out estimates of P_{max} implied by the current regulatory regime.[7] As table 6-1 indicates, the current set of solvency regulations implies a maximum probability of failure for S&Ls that is significantly greater than for other intermediaries. Consequently, S&Ls may select a point on their locus that exposes them to substantially greater risk. Conversely, the current regulatory regime restricts credit unions from exposing themselves to a probability of failure that is greater than 0.0245 percent, which is 66.4 percent less than the maximum probability of failure for S&Ls. Further, the maximum probability of

Table 6-1
"Acceptable" Maximum Probability of Bankruptcy of Depository
Intermediaries under the Current Regulatory Regime
(Percent)

Key Parameters	Commercial Bank	Mutual Savings Bank	S&L	Credit Union	Unconstrained Intermediary
P_{max}	0.0501	0.0572	0.0730	0.0245	0.0330
Risk	2.50	2.50	2.80	1.75	2.00
Return	11.69	4.57	3.70	11.73	10.28

failure for credit unions yields an expected rate of return on capital of 11.73 percent. This is 317 percent greater than the rate of return expected by S&Ls at their maximum probability of failure.

We found in chapter 5 that the current set of regulations appear to favor credit unions and commercial banks over mutual savings banks and S&Ls. That is, both credit unions and commercial banks enjoy superior risk-return loci relative to the loci of the thrift institutions. It is not surprising therefore that both commercial banks and credit unions enjoy the lowest probability of failure. Interestingly, although the current set of regulations imply a lower maximum probability of failure for credit unions than for the unconstrained intermediary, the unconstrained institution is still safer than the remaining intermediaries.

Table 6-2 reports the probability of failure of each intermediary under the current regulatory regime over the entire permissible range of risk.[8] As the table indicates, S&Ls and mutual savings banks exhibit the highest risk of default. In general, the ranking of intermediaries in terms of the probability of failure is identical to the ranking of the intermediaries with respect to their risk-return loci. Thus credit unions and commercial banks are somewhat safer than S&Ls and mutual savings banks. For example, at a risk σ_K of 1.75 percent, the probability of failure for S&Ls is 11.00 percent higher than for commercial banks and 15.00 percent higher than for credit unions.

The data indicate that a percent increase in risk results in a larger percent increase in P. For example, moving from a risk level of 1.25 percent to 1.50 percent amounts to a 20-percent increase in risk. This translates into a 11.51 percent increase in $\bar{R}_K$, a 15.49-percent decrease in the capital-asset ratio, and a 38.57-percent increase in the probability of failure for a commercial bank. The same percent increase in risk translates into a 8.53-percent increase in $\bar{R}_K$, a 14.06-percent decrease in the capital-asset ratio, and a 43.24-percent increase in the probability of failure for S&Ls. Figure 6-3 compares the probability of failure for each intermediary under the current regulatory regime over the entire risk interval.

Table 6-2
**Probability of Bankruptcy of Depository Intermediaries under the Current
Regulatory Regime (Chebychev's Inequality)**
(Percent)

Risk σ_K	Commercial Bank	Mutual Savings Bank	S&L	Credit Union
		Probability		
0.25	0.0006	0.0006	0.0006	0.0006
0.50	0.0023	0.0024	0.0024	0.0022
0.75	0.0051	0.0053	0.0054	0.0049
1.00	0.0089	0.0094	0.0095	0.0084
1.25	0.0140	0.0145	0.0148	0.0129
1.50	0.0194	0.0207	0.0212	0.0184
1.75	0.0259	0.0281	0.0288	0.0245
2.00	0.0332	0.0368	0.0374	
2.25	0.0413	0.0466	0.0473	Infeasible
2.50	0.0501	0.0572	0.0584	
2.75	0.0691	0.0692	0.0704	
Solvency Parameters				
β (%)	7.20	1.80	2.0	0.0
$\bar{R}_D$ (%)	1.21	1.30	1.32	1.35
Risky portfolio	A	A	A	A

Note: See table 5-11, which presents the complete risk-return characteristics of each
intermediary for this regulatory regime.

Sensitivity of the Probability of Bankruptcy
to Changes in Solvency Regulations

As we discussed earlier, P_{max} for each intermediary is determined by the current
set of regulations. We further discussed how P_{max} shifts as one regulatory
standard is changed holding all others constant. One implication is that the
regulatory authorities may shift several standards in opposite directions leaving
the maximum probability of failure unchanged.

Tables 6-3 through 6-5 report the values of P_{max} for each type of
intermediary when several regulations are changed. Table 6-3 presents the values
of P_{max} after asset restrictions are relaxed holding all other regulations constant.
As the data indicate, P_{max} falls by 2.2 percent, 43.95 percent, 4.8 percent and
56.7 percent for commercial banks, mutual savings banks, S&Ls, and credit
unions, respectively. Consequently, this change in regulation has led to a
decrease in the maximum probability of failure without simultaneously raising
capital requirements.

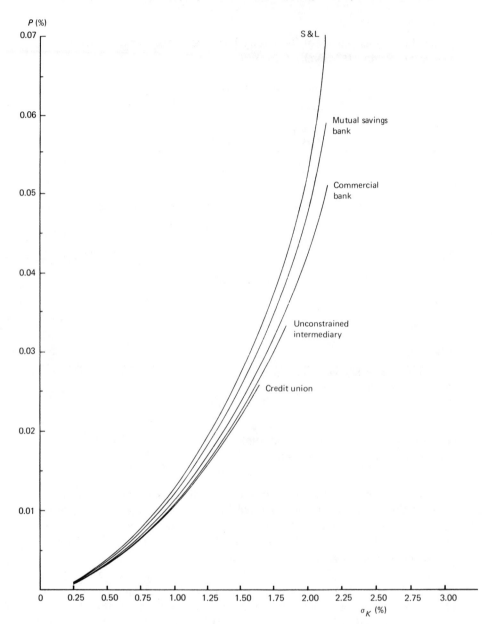

Figure 6-3. Probability of Bankruptcy of Each Intermediary under the Current Regulatory Regime

Table 6-3
Maximum Probability of Bankruptcy of Depository Intermediaries after a Change in Asset Restrictions
(Percent)

Key Parameters	Commercial Bank	Mutual Savings Bank	S&L	Credit Union
P_{max}	0.0490	0.0321	0.0695	0.0143
Risk	2.50	2.00	2.75	1.25
Return	12.0	11.57	4.20	4.55

For the sake of comparison, table 6-4 reports the value of P_{max} for each type of intermediary when the authorities increase the acceptable capital-asset ratio by 5 percent. Although P_{max} is lower in this regime relative to the current regime (with the exception of mutual savings banks), it is higher than the maximum probability of failure that results when asset restrictions are relaxed. It appears therefore that regulators can move closer to their goal of insuring the solidity of the entire industry by relaxing asset restrictions as opposed to raising capital requirements.

Finally, table 6-5 reports the values of P_{max} when asset restrictions and capital requirements shift simultaneously. While the values of P_{max} fall under this regime relative to the current regime, they do not necessarily do so relative to the case when only asset restrictions are changed. This is due primarily to the trade-off between reducing risk as asset restrictions change and increasing risk as an intermediary suboptimally trades off investment exposure for leverage exposure to satisfy the lower leverage constraint.

The examples presented indicate that regulators can achieve their largest gains with a change in asset restrictions; as portfolio restrictions are relaxed, the maximum probability of system failure falls dramatically. Indeed, the current set of regulations imply a higher maximum probability of system failure relative to a regime in which either asset restrictions or leverage constraints change.

Recall from chapter 5 that the risk-return characteristics of each intermediary does not change significantly when required reserves increase by 5 percent. Accordingly, the probability of failure should not change appreciably under this regulatory regime. Table 6-6 indicates that this is indeed the case. Although each intermediary's risk-return locus falls subsequent to a 5-percent increase in required reserves, the fall is so slight as to have only a negligible impact on the probability of failure.

A 5-percent increase in deposit-rate ceilings, on the other hand, raises the probability of failure relative to the preceding regime whether the change in

Table 6-4
Maximum Probability of Bankruptcy of Depository Intermediaries after a
5-percent Increase in the Acceptable Capital-Asset Ratio
(Percent)

Key Parameters	Commercial Bank	Mutual Savings Bank	S&L	Credit Union
P_{max}	0.0413	0.0572	0.0706	0.0185
Risk	2.25	2.50	2.75	1.50
Return	10.69	4.57	3.45	10.43

regulation affects the expected cost of funds or all three key parameters. (See chapter 5 for a discussion of this issue.) As tables 6-7 and 6-8 indicate, at a risk level of 1.50 percent the probability of failure under this regime increases by 1.03 percent, 2.41 percent, 1.89 percent, and 1.63 percent for commercial banks, mutual savings banks, S&Ls, and credit unions, respectively. Although these percentage increases are small, they are significantly greater than the changes induced by the preceding regime. This of course is not surprising given the effect this regime has on the risk-return locus of each intermediary.

Table 6-9 reports the probability of failure when portfolio restrictions and rate ceilings change simultaneously. In general, the probability of failure moves in the same direction as the risk-return locus, regardless of the regulatory regime introduced. Thus the probability of failure of each intermediary will move in the same direction as its respective risk-return locus when this regime is imposed. Recall from chapter 5 that a mutual savings bank's risk-return locus improves significantly when asset restrictions change and deposit-rate ceilings rise. Accordingly, at a risk level of 1.50 percent, the probability of failure for a mutual

Table 6-5
Maximum Probability of Bankruptcy of Depository Intermediaries after a
Change in Asset Restrictions and a 5-percent Increase in the
Acceptable Capital-Asset Ratio
(Percent)

Key Parameters	Commercial Bank	Mutual Savings Bank	S&L	Credit Union
P_{max}	0.0411	0.0214	0.0696	0.0144
Risk	2.25	1.75	2.75	1.25
Return	10.99	10.36	4.20	4.13

Table 6-6
Probability of Bankruptcy of Depository Intermediaries after a 5-percent
Increase in Required Reserves (Chebychev's Inequality)
(Percent)

	Probability			
Risk σ_K	*Commercial* *Bank*	*Mutual* *Savings* *Bank*	*S&L*	*Credit* *Union*
0.25	0.0006	0.0006	0.0006	0.0005
0.50	0.0023	0.0024	0.0024	0.0022
0.75	0.0051	0.0053	0.0054	0.0049
1.00	0.0090	0.0094	0.0095	0.0084
1.25	0.0137	0.0145	0.0148	0.0130
1.50	0.0194	0.0207	0.0212	0.0184
1.75	0.0259	0.0282	0.0287	
2.00	0.0333	0.0368	0.0374	
2.25	0.0414	0.0466	0.0473	Infeasible
2.50	0.0502	0.0571	0.0584	
2.75	0.0692	0.0693	0.0704	
Solvency Parameters				
β (%)	7.6	1.9	2.1	1.0
$\bar{R}_D$ (%)	1.21	1.30	1.32	1.35
Risky portfolio	A	A	A	A

Note: See table 5-12, which presents the complete risk-return characteristics of each
intermediary for this regulatory regime.

savings bank falls by approximately 7 percent. In sharp contrast, the probability
of failure for S&Ls increases by approximately 10 percent at the same risk level.
Finally, the probability of failure increases slightly for both commercial banks
and credit unions when this regime is introduced.

Summary

The probability of bankruptcy of each intermediary under the current regulatory regime is extremely low. Of course, the probability of failure is not the only
important issue; the costs to depositors and to the economy should failure occur
are equally important. The appropriate measure of risk is therefore the expected
cost of failure. However, without some notion of the cost component, such a
calculation is not possible. Nevertheless, the data indicate the degree of risk
regulators impose on the despository intermediary system under the current

Table 6-7

Probability of Bankruptcy of Depository Intermediaries after a 5-percent Increase in Deposit-rate Ceilings (Chebychev's Inequality)
(Percent)

Risk σ_K	Commercial Bank	Mutual Savings Bank	S&L	Credit Union
		Probability		
0.25	0.0006	0.0006	0.0006	0.0005
0.50	0.0023	0.0024	0.0024	0.0023
0.75	0.0052	0.0054	0.0054	0.0049
1.00	0.0090	0.0095	0.0096	0.0086
1.25	0.0138	0.0150	0.0150	0.0132
1.50	0.0196	0.0212	0.0216	0.0187
1.75	0.0262	0.0287	0.0293	0.0251
2.00	0.0337	0.0375	0.0383	
2.25	0.0419	0.0474	0.0483	Infeasible
2.50	0.0588	0.0582	0.0595	
2.75	0.0703	0.0705	0.0720	
Solvency Parameters				
β (%)	7.2	1.8	2.0	0.0
$\bar{R}_D$ (%)	1.258	1.355	1.379	1.417
Risky portfolio	A	A	A	A

Note: See table 5-13, which presents the complete risk-return characteristics of each intermediary for this regulatory regime.

regulatory regime and the risk of default of each type of intermediary relative to an unconstrained intermediary.

The probability of bankruptcy measure is also important in that it provides regulators with some notion of the consequences implied by a particular change in the set of solvency standards. For example, other factors being equal, a small change in reserve requirements results in a negligible change in P; conversely, a small change in deposit-rate ceilings induces an appreciable change in P.

In general, solvency regulations increase the probability of failure relative to the unconstrained regime. Therefore, regulators appear to be moving away from their objective of ensuring the solidity of the depository intermediary system. Perhaps regulators should specify only an "acceptable" maximum upper bound on the probability of bankruptcy and not assign any values to the solvency standards. An intermediary could then choose any investment and leverage exposure, and pay any price for deposits so long as its probability of failure did not violate the regulatory constraint P_{max}.

Table 6-8
Probability of Bankruptcy of Depository Intermediaries after a 5-percent Increase in Deposit-rate Ceilings, with Parameters Shifted Proportionately (Chebychev's Inequality)
(Percent)

Risk σ_K	Probability			
	Commercial Bank	Mutual Savings Bank	S&L	Credit Union
0.25	0.0006	0.0006	0.0006	0.0005
0.50	0.0023	0.0024	0.0024	0.0022
0.75	0.0052	0.0053	0.0054	0.0050
1.00	0.0090	0.0095	0.0096	0.0087
1.25	0.0138	0.0147	0.0150	0.0133
1.50	0.0196	0.0211	0.0216	0.0189
1.75	0.0262	0.0287	0.0293	0.0254
2.00	0.0336	0.0374	0.0382	
2.25	0.0419	0.0474	0.0483	Infeasible
2.50	0.0508	0.0583	0.0595	
2.75	0.0710	0.0705	0.0719	
Solvency Parameters				
β (%)	7.2	1.8	2.0	0.6
$\bar{R}_D$ (%)	1.258	1.355	1.379	1.417
Risky portfolio	A	A	A	A

Note: See table 5-14, which presents the complete risk-return characteristics of each intermediary for this regulatory regime.

Table 6-9
Probability of Bankruptcy of Depository Intermediaries after a 5-percent Increase in Rate Ceilings and a Relaxation of Portfolio Restrictions
(Chebychev's Inequality)
(Percent)

Risk σ_K	Probability			
	Commercial Bank	Mutual Savings Bank	S&L	Credit Union
0.25	0.0006	0.0006	0.0006	0.0006
0.50	0.0023	0.0023	0.0024	0.0022
0.75	0.0051	0.0051	0.0054	0.0049
1.00	0.0089	0.0089	0.0096	0.0085
1.25	0.0138	0.0136	0.0150	0.0130
1.50	0.0195	0.0192	0.0214	
1.75	0.0261	0.0256	0.0291	
2.00	0.0335	0.0329	0.0380	Infeasible
2.25	0.0420		0.0478	
2.50	0.0505	Infeasible	0.0589	
2.75	0.0710		0.0710	
Solvency Parameters				
β (%)	7.2	1.8	2.0	0.0
$\bar{R}_D$ (%)	1.258	1.355	1.379	1.417
Risky portfolio	D	C	C'	E

Note: See table 5-15, which presents the complete risk-return characteristics of each intermediary for this regulatory regime.

Notes

1. One might argue that solvency regulation has succeeded in reducing the probability of failure since the number of institutions that actually fail is quite small (less than 0.1 percent of the insured deposits failed over the period 1970-1974). However, since the FDIC or FSLIC normally intervenes before an intermediary actually fails, the small number of observed bankruptcies is not indicative of the effects of solvency regulation.

2. R. Blair and A. Heggestad, "Bank Portfolio Regulation and the Probability of Bank Failure," use Chebychev's inequality to examine the effect of asset restrictions on the probability of intermediary failure. They did not, however, generalize their model to examine the simultaneous effects of solvency regulations, nor did they offer any estimates of these effects. The original formulation is from A. Roy, "Safety First and the Holding of Assets."

3. Chebychev's inequality states

$$P_r\left(|\tilde{R}_N - \bar{R}_N| > q\sigma_N\right) < \frac{1}{q^2}$$

The focus of attention is on bankruptcy, thus

$$P_r(\tilde{R}_N < \overline{R}_N - q\sigma_N) < \frac{1}{q^2}$$

If $b = \overline{R}_N - q\sigma_N$ = point of bankruptcy = $-(1/1 + L)$, then

$$q = \frac{\overline{R}_N - b}{\sigma_N}$$

Substituting the definition of q into Chebychev's inequality yields (equation 6.3)

$$P_r(\tilde{R}_N < b) \leqslant \frac{\sigma_N^2}{(\overline{R}_N - b)^2} = P$$

Multiplying equation 6.2 by $(1 + L)$ indicates that bankruptcy occurs whenever the rate of return on invested capital is less than -1. Substituting this expression into Chebychev's inequality yields the probability of failure in terms of $\overline{R}_K$ and σ_K, namely (equation 6.3'),

$$P_r(R_K < -1) \leqslant \frac{\sigma_K^2}{(\overline{R}_K + 1)^2} = P$$

4. If we assume that the rate of return on the risky portfolio and the cost of funds are both normally distributed, we can measure the probability of insolvency with much greater precision. Using the definition of bankruptcy, equation 6.2, and assuming normality yields

$$P_r(\tilde{R}_N < b) = \Phi\left(\frac{b - \overline{R}_N}{\sigma_N}\right) \qquad (6.4)$$

where

Φ = the cumulative density function of the unit normal distribution.

Examination of this equation indicates that each solvency instrument operates in identical fashion as in equation 6.3.

5. The "acceptable" maximum upper bound on the probability of failure can be found by substituting L_{max}, the other parameters of solvency regulation, and the corresponding optimal value of α_R into equation 6.3.

6. An iso-P locus in risk-return on invested capital space $(\bar{R}_K, \sigma_K)$ is a ray with intercept -1 and slope $(\bar{R}_K + 1)/\sigma_K$ (see footnote 3). The inverse of the slope of this ray squared is the upper bound P. As the slope of the ray increases, the upper bound on the probability of failure decreases. See A. Roy, "Safety First and the Holding of Assets."

7. For our purposes, the maximum probability of failure of each intermediary under the current regulatory regime is determined by the maximum risk level that an intermediary can assume on its risk-return locus while still increasing its rate of return. Certainly, the firm will not move past this point on its locus since it could improve its return by simply reducing its scale.

8. Specifically, the probability of failure was estimated at several points on the risk-return locus between the risk interval 0.25 to 2.75.

7 Summary of Results

This study was undertaken to determine how solvency regulations affect the risk-return locus and the probability of bankruptcy of each type of intermediary. Solvency regulations are defined as those regulatory instruments designed to protect the capital of a depository intermediary.

In general, the justification given for the regulation of depository intermediaries is that failure not only affects the owners of these firms but also their depositors. Moreover, bankruptcy of an intermediary may also affect the payments mechanism and therefore the health of the economy. Failure of a depository intermediary therefore produces costs that capital does not bear alone.

The solvency instruments analyzed in this study are portfolio restrictions (that is, asset restrictions and reserve requirements), deposit-rate ceilings, and capital adequacy requirements. It is generally felt that each instrument, in isolation, reduces the risk of insolvency. Specifically, assets restrictions eliminate what are thought to be too risky securities from the investment opportunity set. Regulation Q-type restrictions protect the capital of an intermediary by ensuring to a certain extent a positive interest-rate spread under most economic conditions. Capital adequacy requirements presumably protect depositors by ensuring that an intermediary has sufficient capital to offset any capital losses that may result from either loan default or sale of marketable securities.

The analysis has shown, however, that each solvency instrument may produce undesirable effects. In general, asset restrictions produce only negative effects while deposit-rate ceilings and capital regulations produce both positive and negative effects. Asset restrictions do not permit recognition that a large number of available assets lead to a reduction of risk through diversification of the portfolio. If regulators look at the standard deviation of the rate of return of a particular asset only and not its covariance properties, a risk-diversifying asset may be excluded inadvertently from the investment opportunity set. The overall effect of asset restrictions is to increase the probability of bankruptcy. Deposit-rate ceilings, on the other hand, permit favorable borrowing rates for an intermediary. As a consequence, this regulation appears to protect the firm from insolvency. However, the variance of the cost of funds may increase significantly under a deposit-rate ceiling regime relative to an unconstrained regime; the overall risk of the firm may possibly rise because of Regulation Q ceilings. Finally, capital regulation serves to protect depositors from the loss of funds by constraining an intermediary from operating on the high-risk portion of its locus.

Nonetheless, if the firm is unable to offset the effects of asset restrictions, it may not provide the return required by its owners.

The net effect of these regulations appears to reduce profitability, increase total risk, and increase the probability of failure of a depository intermediary relative to the unconstrained regime. If this overall effect is significant, then the industry may have difficulty raising capital to support any level of deposits. This in turn will reduce the quantity of funds available for real investment, and the growth of the real economy may suffer.

We began the analysis by introducing a simple financial model of an intermediary. Using this model we compared the risk-return opportunities facing a constrained intermediary to those of an unconstrained intermediary. Depending on the severity of solvency regulations, an intermediary may be unable to earn a risk-adjusted expected rate of return that is approximately equal to the rate of return promised in the unconstrained regime.

Unless the values of the market and solvency parameters are known, one cannot determine a priori the extent to which an intermediary is affected by each solvency regulation. After estimating the values of these parameters, we examined each regulation to determine its impact on each type of depository intermediary.

Although asset restrictions were found to lower the risk-return locus of each type of intermediary, S&Ls and mutual savings banks were most severely affected by these regulations relative to credit unions and commercial banks. Deposit-rate ceilings on balance raise the risk-return locus of each intermediary; however, S&Ls and mutual savings banks are unable to offset the negative impacts of asset restrictions. Reserve requirements, on the other hand, reduce the profitability of each intermediary but not to the extent of asset restrictions. Finally, leverage constraints restrict the operating area of a credit union to a much greater extent than for the other intermediaries.

We found that the ranking of the risk-return loci and the risk of insolvency are identical. In general, commercial banks and credit unions enjoy the most favorable set of solvency regulations in that their risk-return loci approximated the locus of an unconstrained intermediary. Consequently, the risk of insolvency was lowest for commerical banks and credit unions and highest for mutual savings banks and S&Ls.

Although the short portfolio horizon may bias the empirical results toward commercial banks and credit unions, the results reported appear to be indicative of the effects of solvency regulation. Asset restrictions adversely affect the probability of default. Regulation Q ceilings protect an intermediary, but these ceilings could be eliminated if asset restrictions were also eliminated. Reserve requirements also increase the probability of insolvency, yet their impact is small relative to asset restrictions. Finally, leverage constraints have only a negligible effect on the probability of failure relative to the unconstrained regime.

The analysis also showed that regulatory reform can be successful only if all restrictions are changed or eliminated simultaneously. Such change in regulation would lead to an improvement of the risk-return characteristics of the major types of depository intermediaries. As a result, each intermediary would be able to bid successfully for its share of capital and the risk of system failure would decline significantly. Further, if these restrictions were relaxed and made uniform across each intermediary, competition between these firms would increase, which in turn would improve the financial services provided to both borrowers and depositors.

Appendix A
Intermediary Response
to Changes in Solvency
Regulation

The primary focus of this study is the risk-return opportunities of a depository intermediary and how these opportunities are influenced by solvency regulation. In this appendix, we will shift our focus to an analysis of the reaction of an intermediary to *changes* in solvency regulation.[1] We will assume, as in the text, that the firm selects a particular point on its risk-return locus on the basis of expected utility with end-of-period return to capital as the argument. The firm selects the point on the locus with respect to two decision variables; namely α_R, the investment exposure of the firm, and L, the leverage exposure of the firm.

For example, assume that the current set of regulations fixes the operating area of the risk-return locus to be AB in figure A-1. The firm will choose a point on this locus that maximizes its expected utility. Specifically, it will select a point where its marginal rate of substitution between risk σ_K and return $\bar{R}_K$ and the slope of the locus is equal (say, point C in figure A-1). As a result of the firm's choosing the risk-return combination C, its probability of failure is $P < P_{\max}$.

As each solvency regulation is changed, the operating area of the risk-return locus shifts respectively. For example, say that asset restrictions are eliminated so that the locus moves up to $A'B'$. The firm may not react to this change; accordingly, it would select point C' on the $A'B'$ locus, which is identical to point C in terms of risk-return characteristics (that is, the slopes are equal). In this case the probability of failure falls below P. On the other hand, the firm may react to the change in regulation and select point D' on the $A'B'$ locus. Now the probability of failure for the firm is greater than P but still less than $P_{\max}$. Consequently, a change in regulation that improved the risk-return opportunities of an intermediary has induced a reaction that exposes the firm to a higher probability of default.

The purpose of this appendix is to analyze the direction of change of the two decision variables of the firm when several important solvency regulations change. This analysis will give some indication of whether changes in solvency regulation may induce an intermediary to increase or decrease its risk-taking.

To carry out this analysis, we will assume that the risk preferences of the firm can be represented by an exponential utility function that exhibits constant absolute risk aversion and increasing proportional risk aversion. For simplicity, we will also assume that the rate of return on the risky portfolio and the average cost of funds are normally distributed.[2] Since maximizing expected utility is identical to maximizing the certainty equivalent, the analysis will focus on the certainty equivalent of end-of-period rate of return.

127

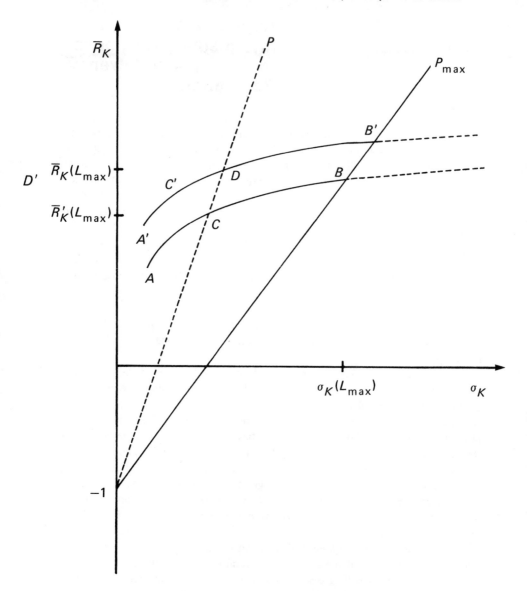

Figure A-1. Optimal Risk-Return Combinations under Different Regulatory Regimes

The certainty equivalent of an exponential utility function assuming normality is[3]

$$CE = \overline{R}_K - \tfrac{1}{2}\gamma\sigma_K^2 \qquad (A.1)$$

where

γ = coefficient of risk aversion. If the firm is risk averse, $\gamma > 0$.

Differentiating equation A.1 with respect to α_R and L and rearranging yields the following first-order conditions for the equilibrium of the firm

$$(\bar{R}_R - R_o) - \gamma \left[\alpha_R \left[1 + L(1 - \beta)\right] \sigma_R^2 - L \, \text{COV} \right] = 0 \qquad (A.2)$$

$$R_o(1 - \beta) - (\bar{R}_D + L\bar{R}_{D_L}) - \gamma [L\sigma_D^2 + \tfrac{1}{2}L^2\sigma_{D_L}^2 \\ - \alpha_R \, \text{COV} \left[1 + L(1 - \beta)\right] \Big] = 0 \qquad (A.3)$$

where

$\text{COV} = \rho\sigma_{R_D}\sigma_R$ (assumed to be greater than 0).

$$\left. \begin{aligned} \sigma_{D_L}^2 &= \frac{\partial \sigma_{R_D}^2}{\partial L} > 0 \\[2mm] \bar{R}_{D_L} &= \frac{\partial \bar{R}_D}{\partial L} > 0 \end{aligned} \right\} \quad \text{See chapter 3.}$$

Equations A.2 and A.3 are intuitively pleasing. In equilibrium, the firm will select an optimal combination of α_R and L such that the marginal risk-adjusted rate spread between the risky portfolio and the risk-free asset, and the marginal risk-adjusted rate spread between the risk-free asset and average cost of funds are both zero.[4]

To determine how the optimality conditions shift with changes in several important solvency regulations, we must take the differential of equations A.2 and A.3 with respect to α_R, L, R_T (the deposit-rate ceiling), β (reserve ratio), and σ_R^2 (a change in asset restrictions).

Setting $d\bar{R}_T = d\sigma_R^2 = 0$, we obtain the change in α_R and L with respect to a small change in the reserve requirement β

$$\frac{dL}{d\beta} = \frac{-[1 + L(1 - \beta)] \, \sigma_R^2 R_o}{D} < 0 \qquad (A.4)$$

$$\frac{d\alpha_R}{d\beta} = \frac{\alpha_R \sigma_R^2 [R_o(1 - \beta) + 2L\bar{R}_{D_L} + \gamma 2L^2\sigma_{D_L}^2 + L\gamma\sigma_D^2(1 - \rho^2)] - R_o \, \text{COV}}{D} > 0$$

$$(A.5)$$

where[5]

$$D = [1 + L(1 - \beta)] \sigma_R^2 [2\overline{R}_{D_L} + 2L\sigma_{D_L}^2 + \gamma\sigma_D^2(1 - \rho^2)] > 0$$

Equations A.4 and A.5 are also intuitively appealing. Since β is an implicit cost of deposits, a higher β reduces the advantage gained from leverage. However, the firm will try to offset the loss of income resulting from the higher price of deposits and the falling leverage by shifting a larger proportion of the remaining total available funds into the risky portfolio. Whether overall risk falls is not clear, however, and will depend on the variance/covariance structure of the risky assets and the cost of funds.

Holding β and σ_R^2 constant, we obtain the change in α_R and L with respect to a change in the deposit-rate ceiling R_T. Thus

$$\frac{dL}{dR_T} = \frac{-[1 + L(1 - \beta)] \sigma_R^2 (\overline{R}_{D_T} + \gamma L\sigma_{D_T}^2)}{D} > 0 \qquad (A.6)$$

$$\frac{d\alpha_R}{dR_T} = \frac{(\overline{R}_{D_T} + \gamma L\sigma_{D_T}^2)[\alpha_R(1 - \beta)\sigma_R^2 - COV]}{D} > 0 \quad (\text{assuming } \overline{R}_{D_T} > \sigma_{D_T}^2)$$

$$(A.7)$$

where

$$\overline{R}_{D_T} = \frac{\partial \overline{R}_D}{\partial R_T} > 0$$

$$\left. \begin{array}{c} \\ \\ \end{array} \right\} \quad \text{See chapter 3.}$$

$$\sigma_{D_T}^2 = \frac{\partial \sigma_D^2}{\partial R_T} < 0$$

The firm reacts to a change in deposit-rate ceilings in the same way it does to a change in reserve requirements. This is not surprising, however, since both R_T and β represent either an explicit or implicit cost of deposits.

Finally, holding R_T and β constant, we obtain the change in α_R and L when asset restrictions are changed. Recall from chapter 3 that asset restrictions result in raising σ_R^2 for a given $\overline{R}_R$. Accordingly, if regulators permit intermediaries to invest in a broader range of assets, we would then expect that σ_R^2 would fall for a given $\overline{R}_R$.

$$\frac{dL}{d\sigma_R^2} = \frac{-\gamma COV [1 + L(1 - \beta)]^2}{D} < 0 \qquad (A.8)$$

$$\frac{d\alpha_R}{d\sigma_R^2} = \frac{-\alpha_R\left[1 + L(1-\beta)\right]\ \left\{2\bar{R}_{D_L} + \gamma\left[\sigma_D^2 + 2L\sigma_{D_L}^2 - \alpha_R\ \text{COV}\,(1-\beta)\right]\right\}}{D} < 0$$

$$(\text{A.9})$$

As equations A.8 and A.9 indicate, if the riskiness of the portfolio falls for a given $\bar{R}_R$, the firm will borrow more funds in which to invest and invest a larger proportion of these funds in the risky portfolio. Whether this reaction will increase the total risk of the firm depends on the variance/covariance structure of the portfolio and cost of funds and the risk-aversion coefficient of the firm. Yet the total risk of the firm could rise after a change in this regulation. Nonetheless, this probability would always lie below $P_{\max}$.

Although the focus of this study is the effect solvency regulations have on the risk-return opportunities and the probability of failure of the firm, we have briefly examined the reaction of the firm to changes in several solvency parameters. Our results were intuitive. Of course, regulators are not only concerned with how regulations affect the firm's total risk but also with how the firm may react to these regulations. As the discussion in the text emphasized, asset restrictions and reserve requirements adversely affect the firm. However, if the authorities relax reserve requirements (asset restrictions), an intermediary (assuming an exponential utility function) may leverage more (more) and invest relatively less (more) funds in the risky portfolio. The net change in the risk of the firm prior to the change in regulation relative to the new regime is not clear. Conceivably, the firm may actually be riskier after the change in either regulation.[6]

We also found in the text that Regulation Q ceilings improve the risk-return locus of the firm. If these ceilings are lowered further, we found that the intermediary may increase leverage but decrease the relative amount of funds invested in risky securities. This follows since the firm does not have to assume a very risky portfolio to earn an adequate return.

Finally, it is interesting to examine the effect on L if the regulator removes asset restrictions and simultaneously lowers reserve requirements. Differentiating equation A.8 with respect to β leads to

$$\frac{d\left(\dfrac{dL}{d\sigma_R^2}\right)}{d\beta} = \frac{\gamma\,\text{COV}\,L}{\sigma_R^2\left[2\bar{R}_{D_L} + 2L\sigma_{D_L}^2 + \gamma\sigma_D^2(1-\rho^2)\right]} > 0 \quad (\text{A.10})$$

Recall that the leverage of the firm rises when asset restrictions are eliminated (that is, reducing σ_R^2 for a given $\bar{R}_R$). If regulators simultaneously lower β, the firm may further raise L beyond the point it would if β were constant. A change in these solvency parameters therefore reinforces each other.

Notes

1. The analysis presented in this appendix is a special case of M.F. Koehn and A.M. Santomero, "Regulation of Bank Capital and Portfolio Risk." Specifically, we assume in this appendix that the preferences of the firm can be represented by an exponential utility function. Koehn and Santomero generalize the analysis by making no assumptions about the form of the preference function.

2. About 55 percent of the ex-post rate-of-return distributions in this study approximated normal distributions. Using the Studentized Range Test, we could not reject the hypothesis that the ex-post rate of return distributions were normal (.05 significance level) (see chapter 4). This assumption therefore does not appear to be overly restrictive.

3. See J. Lintner, "The Valuation of Risk Assets and the Selection of Risky Investments in Stock Portfolios and Capital Budgets," *Review of Economics and Statistics* 47 (1965):13-37.

4. Note that the second-order conditions for a maximum are satisfied; namely, $CE_{\alpha_R \alpha_R} < 0$ and $CE_{\alpha_R \alpha_R} CE_{LL} - (CE_{L\alpha_R})^2 > 0$.

5. For simplicity, we assume that the covariance between the risky portfolio and the cost of funds does not change with L or R_T. We also assume that the cross-product derivatives are all zero (for example, $\overline{R}_{D_{LR_T}} = 0$). These assumptions do not affect our results.

6. Koehn and Santomero demonstrate that the risk of an intermediary may indeed rise as certain regulations are changed.

Appendix B
Estimation of
Loan-Loss Rates

**Regression Equations to Estimate Quarterly Loan Losses for
Six Categories of Loans Using Annual Data**

| | Independent Variable[b] | | | |
Dependent Variable Losses	GNP	Unemployment Rate	Intercept	R^2
Mortgage (FHA and FHLBB)	.00002 (3.83)	a	.01172	.7095
Automobile loans	a	.04669 (2.62)	.20425	.5327
Personal loans	a	.20453 (4.72)	.10151	.7876
Mobile home loans	.00083 (5.52)	a	−.80825	.8354
Other consumer loans	a	.12363 (3.27)	−.08983	.6401
Commercial loans	.00012 (4.94)	a	.12018	.8026

[a]The corresponding independent variable was not used in the estimating equation.

[b]All t-values in parentheses are significant at the .025 level or lower.

Appendix C

Risk-Return Characteristics of an Unconstrained Depository Intermediary
(Percent)

σ_K	$\bar{R}_K$	$\dfrac{1}{1+L}$	α_R	P
0.25	3.11	26.31	100.00	0.0005
0.50	4.16	15.87	100.00	0.0023
0.75	5.20	11.50	100.00	0.0051
1.00	6.21	9.10	100.00	0.0089
1.25	7.23	7.50	100.00	0.0136
1.50	8.25	6.33	100.00	0.0192
1.75	9.26	5.53	100.00	0.0256
2.00	10.28	4.88	100.00	0.0329
2.25	8.73	4.85	83.25	0.0429
2.50	7.52	4.81	70.00	0.0541
2.75	6.25	4.83	56.67	0.0700

Solvency Parameters

$\beta\ (\%)\ = 0$

$R_D\quad = R_S$

$L_{\max}\ = 20$

Appendix D
Efficient Frontiers under Various Asset Restrictions

This appendix presents each intermediary's efficient investment frontiers as additional assets are introduced into its investment opportunity set. The efficient frontiers derived under the current regulatory regime are presented in chapter 5. The frontiers derived under the regime where asset restrictions are almost entirely eliminated are also presented in chapter 5. Thus the results reported in this appendix lie between these two extremes. The efficient frontiers are presented in tables D-1 to D-12.

Table D-1
Commercial Bank Investment Frontier B
(Percentage Composition of Efficient Portfolios)

	1	2	3	4	5	6	7	8	9
A1	–	–	–	–	–	–	–		
A2	–	–	–	–	–	–	–		
A3	–	–	–	–	–	–	–		
A4	–	–	–	–	–	–	–		
A5	4.8	2.0	–	–	–	–	–		
A6	–	0.4	1.1	–	–	–	–		
A7	69.8	77.3	83.0	–	–	–	–		
A8	–	–	–	–	–	–	–		
A9	6.0	1.4	–	–	–	–	–		
A10	7.8	10.1	13.1	95.0	70.0	45.0	20.0		
A11	1.1	1.1	0.7	–	–	–	–		
A12	–	–	–	–	–	–	–	Infeasible	
A13	4.5	3.3	–	–	–	–	–		
A14	0.8	1.0	0.8	–	–	–	–		
A15	0.2	0.4	0.8	–	–	–	–		
A16*	–	–	–	–	–	–	–		
A17*	–	–	–	–	–	–	–		
A18*	–	–	–	–	–	–	–		
A19	4.9	3.0	–	–	–	–	–		
A20	–	–	0.2	5.0	30.0	55.0	80.0		
A21	–	0.1	0.1	–	–	–	–		
A22*	–	–	–	–	–	–	–		
A23*	–	–	–	–	–	–	–		
A24*	–	–	–	–	–	–	–		
A25*	–	–	–	–	–	–	–		
Portfolio return (%)	1.80	1.85	1.90	1.95	2.00	2.05	2.10		
Standard deviation (%)	0.12	0.14	0.15	0.38	1.36	2.51	3.70		
Shadow price	0.16	0.31	0.10	3.33	30.76	58.18	85.61		

*Indicates assets excluded from the investment opportunity set.

Table D-2

Commercial Bank Investment Frontier C

(Percentage Composition of Efficient Portfolios)

	1	2	3	4	5	6	7	8	9
A1	–	–	–	–	–	–	–		
A2	–	–	–	–	–	–	–		
A3	–	–	–	–	–	–	–		
A4	–	–	–	–	–	–	–		
A5	5.8	4.5	–	–	–	–	–		
A6	–	–	–	–	–	–	–		
A7	62.4	67.2	74.9	9.3	–	–	–		
A8	–	–	–	–	–	–	–		
A9	6.5	2.7	–	–	–	–	–		
A10	7.7	8.5	8.4	46.0	–	–	–		
A11	1.0	1.0	0.9	–	–	–	–		
A12	–	–	–	–	–	–	–		
A13	3.7	2.5	1.4	–	–	–	–	Infeasible	
A14	–	–	–	–	–	–	–		
A15	0.5	0.8	1.0	–	–	–	–		
A16	2.7	1.9	0.5	–	–	–	–		
A17	–	–	–	–	–	–	–		
A18*	–	–	–	–	–	–	–		
A19	1.2	10.9	–	–	–	–	–		
A20	–	–	0.1	2.1	22.2	50.0	77.8		
A21	–	–	–	–	–	–	–		
A22	8.6	–	12.9	42.6	77.8	50.0	22.2		
A23	–	–	–	–	–	–	–		
A24*	–	–	–	–	–	–	–		
A25*	–	–	–	–	–	–	–		
Portfolio return (%)	1.80	1.85	1.90	1.95	2.00	2.05	2.10		
Standard deviation (%)	0.12	0.12	0.13	0.27	1.11	2.33	3.60		
Shadow price	0.01	0.23	0.04	1.60	25.87	58.36	90.85		

*Indicates assets excluded from the investment opportunity set.

As we might expect, when additional assets are introduced into each intermediary's investment opportunity set, the risk-return trade-off improves relative to the current regulatory regime. However, the investment frontier of mutual savings banks and S&Ls improves significantly when all types of short-term consumer loans are introduced into their feasible sets. This may be due to the short-term portfolio horizon assumed in this study; yet it is indicative of the disadvantage thrift institutions have regarding their investment alternatives and the significant improvement in risk and return as asset restrictions are relaxed.

Table D-3
Mutual Savings Bank Investment Frontier B
(Percentage Composition of Efficient Portfolios)

	1	2	3	4	5	6	7	8	9
A1	—	—	—	—	—	—	—	—	—
A2	—	—	—	—	—	—	—	—	—
A3	—	—	—	—	—	—	—	—	—
A4	—	—	—	—	—	—	—·	—	—
A5*	—	—	—	—	—	—	—	—	—
A6*	—	—	—	—	—	—	—	—	—
A7	70.3	77.7	83.5	41.8	—	—	—	—	—
A8	—	—	—	—	—	—	—	—	—
A9	8.2	1.3	—	—	—	—	—	—	—
A10	6.4	9.4	12.6	54.3	80.2	82.3	74.5	66.6	58.7
A11	0.6	0.6	0.3	—	—	—	—	—	—
A12	—	—	—	—	—	—	—	—	—
A13	6.5	5.1	1.4	—	—	—	—	—	—
A14	0.5	0.8	0.7	—	—	—	—	—	—
A15	—	0.2	0.7	—	—	—	—	—	—
A16*	—	—	—	—	—	—	—	—	—
A17*	—	—	—	—	—	—	—	—	—
A18*	—	—	—	—	—	—	—	—	—
A19	7.1	4.7	—	—	—	—	—	—	—
A20	—	—	0.2	1.5	3.2	5.4	7.7	9.9	12.2
A21	—	—	—	—	—	—	—	—	—
A22*	—	—	—	—	—	—	—	—	—
A23*	—	—	—	—	—	—	—	—	—
A24*	—	—	—	—	—	—	—	—	—
A25	—	0.3	0.4	2.4	6.6	12.2	17.9	23.5	28.1
Portfolio return (%)	1.80	1.85	1.90	1.95	2.00	2.05	2.10	2.15	2.20
Standard deviation (%)	0.12	0.13	0.15	0.24	0.54	1.00	1.50	1.99	2.49
Shadow price	0.01	0.02	0.06	1.08	4.46	9.61	14.76	19.90	25.04

*Indicates assets excluded from the investment opportunity set.

Table D-4
S&L Investment Frontier B
(Percentage Composition of Efficient Portfolios)

	1	2	3	4	5	6	7	8	9
A1	—	—	—						
A2	—	—	—						
A3	—	—	—						
A4	—	—	—						
A5*	—	—	—						
A6*	—	—	—						
A7	—	—	—						
A8	—	—	—						
A9	—	—	—						
A10	20.0	20.0	8.0						
A11	21.1	7.2	—						
A12	58.9	72.8	80.0			Infeasible			
A13	—	—	—						
A14	—	—	—						
A15	—	—	—						
A16*	—	—	—						
A17*	—	—	—						
A18*	—	—	—						
A19	—	—	—						
A20	—	—	12.0						
A21	—	—	—						
A22*	—	—	—						
A23*	—	—	—						
A24*	—	—	—						
A25*	—	—	—						
Portfolio return (%)	1.80	1.85	1.90						
Standard deviation (%)	3.22	3.71	4.34						
Shadow price	29.67	37.90	68.17						

Indicates assets excluded from the investment opportunity set.

Table D-5
S&L Investment Frontier C
(Percentage Composition of Efficient Portfolios)

	1	2	3	4	5	6	7	8	9
A1	—	—	—	—					
A2	—	—	—	—					
A3	—	—	—	—					
A4	—	—	—	—					
A5	—	—	—	—					
A6	—	—	—	—					
A7	—	—	—	—					
A8	—	—	—	—					
A9	—	—	—	—					
A10	—	—	—	—					
A11	42.4	33.9	20.0	6.1					
A12	37.6	46.1	60.0	73.9		Infeasible			
A13	—	—	—	—					
A14	—	—	—	—					
A15	—	—	—	—					
A16	—	—	—	—					
A17	—	—	—	—					
A18	—	—	—	—					
A19	—	—	—	—					
A20	—	—	—	—					
A21	—	—	—	—					
A22	4.2	—	—	—					
A23	—	—	—	—					
A24	15.8	20.0	20.0	20.0					
A25*	—	—	—	—					
Portfolio return (%)	1.80	1.85	1.90	1.95					
Standard deviation (%)	3.05	3.44	3.89	4.39					
Shadow price	22.42	29.04	37.27	45.50					

*Indicates assets excluded from the investment opportunity set.

Table D-6
S&L Investment Frontier D
(Percentage Composition of Efficient Portfolios)

	1	2	3	4	5	6	7	8	9
A1	–	–	–	–	–				
A2	–	–	–	–	–				
A3	–	–	–	–	–				
A4	–	–	–	–	–				
A5	–	–	–	–	–				
A6	–	–	–	–	–				
A7	–	–	–	–	–				
A8	–	–	–	–	–				
A9	–	–	–	–	–				
A10	–	–	–	–	–				
A11	44.1	39.0	28.6	18.1	7.7				
A12	35.9	41.0	51.4	61.9	72.3		Infeasible		
A13	–	–	–	–	–				
A14	–	–	–	–	–				
A15	–	–	–	–	–				
A16	–	–	–	–	–				
A17	–	–	–	–	–				
A18	–	–	–	–	–				
A19	–	–	–	–	–				
A20	–	–	–	–	–				
A21	–	–	–	–	–				
A22	4.4	–	–	–	–				
A23	–	–	–	–	–				
A24	13.4	14.4	10.6	6.9	3.1				
A25	2.2	5.6	9.4	13.1	16.9				
Portfolio return (%)	1.80	1.85	1.90	1.95	2.00				
Standard deviation (%)	3.04	3.40	3.78	4.20	4.63				
Shadow price	21.03	24.96	30.46	35.95	41.45				

Table D-7
S&L Investment Frontier A with 4.5-percent Liquidity Constraint
(Percentage Composition of Efficient Portfolios)

	1	2	3	4	5	6	7	8	9
A1	–	–							
A2	4.5	4.5							
A3	–	–							
A4	–	–							
A5*	–	–							
A6*	–	–							
A7	–	–							
A8*	–	–							
A9*	–	–							
A10*	–	–							
A11	26.2	12.3							
A12	53.8	67.7				Infeasible			
A13	–	–							
A14	–	–							
A15	–	–							
A16*	–	–							
A17*	–	–							
A18*	–	–							
A19	–	–							
A20	15.5	15.5							
A21	–	–							
A22*	–	–							
A23*	–	–							
A24*	–	–							
A25*	–	–							
Portfolio return (%)	1.80	1.85							
Standard deviation (%)	3.49	3.97							
Shadow price	31.55	39.78							

*Indicates assets excluded from the investment opportunity set.

Table D-8
S&L Investment Frontier A'
(Percentage Composition of Efficient Portfolios)

	1	2	3	4	5	6	7	8	9
A1	–	–	–	–	–				
A2	–	–	–	–	–				
A3	–	–	–	–	–				
A4	–	–	–	–	–				
A5*	–	–	–	–	–				
A6*	–	–	–	–	–				
A7	–	–	–	–	–				
A8	–	–	–	–	–				
A9	–	–	–	–	–				
A10	60.0	60.0	60.0	39.0	14.0				
A11	30.0	16.1	2.2	–	–				
A12	10.0	23.9	37.8	40.0	40.0		Infeasible		
A13	–	–	–	–	–				
A14	–	–	–	–	–				
A15	–	–	–	–	–				
A16*	–	–	–	–	–				
A17*	–	–	–	–	–				
A18*	–	–	–	–	–				
A19	–	–	–	–	–				
A20	–	–	–	21.0	46.0				
A21	–	–	–	–	–				
A22*	–	–	–	–	–				
A23*	–	–	–	–	–				
A24*	–	–	–	–	–				
A25*	–	–	–	–	–				
Portfolio return (%)	1.80	1.85	1.90	1.95	2.00				
Standard deviation (%)	1.14	1.49	1.98	2.73	3.71				
Shadow price	4.88	13.11	21.34	49.47	76.29				

Note: 40-percent mortgage constant.

*Indicates assets excluded from the investment opportunity set.

Table D-9
S&L Investment Frontier B$'$
(Percentage Composition of Efficient Portfolios)

	1	2	3	4	5	6	7	8	9
A1	—	—	—	—	—	—	—	—	
A2	—	—	—	—	—	—	—	—	
A3	—	—	—	—	—	—	—	—	
A4	—	—	—	—	—	—	—	—	
A5	—	—	—	—	—	—	—	—	
A6	—	—	—	—	—	—	—	—	
A7	—	—	—	—	—	—	—	—	
A8	—	—	—	—	—	—	—	—	
A9	—	—	—	—	—	—	—	—	
A10	56.9	17.2	—	—	—	—	—	—	
A11	34.1	25.2	17.2	11.7	5.5	—	—	—	
A12	85.9	14.2	22.2	28.3	34.5	40.0	40.0	40.0	Infeasible
A13	—	—	—	—	—	—	—	—	
A14	—	—	—	—	—	—	—	—	
A15	—	—	—	—	—	—	—	—	
A16	—	—	—	—	—	—	—	—	
A17	—	—	—	—	—	—	—	—	
A18	—	—	—	—	—	—	—	—	
A19	—	—	—	—	—	—	—	—	
A20	—	—	—	—	—	—	—	—	
A21	—	—	—	—	—	—	—	—	
A22	—	37.4	50.4	44.3	38.3	31.7	20.9	10.0	
A23	—	—	—	—	—	—	—	—	
A24	3.1	5.2	9.6	15.7	21.7	28.3	39.1	50.0	
A25*	—	—	—	—	—	—	—	—	
Portfolio return (%)	1.80	1.85	1.90	1.95	2.00	2.05	2.10	2.15	
Standard deviation (%)	1.13	1.37	1.74	2.18	2.65	3.15	3.67	4.22	
Shadow price	3.52	8.64	14.21	20.10	26.00	32.02	39.38	46.74	

Note: 40-percent mortgage constant.
*Indicates assets excluded from the investment opportunity set.

Table D-10
Credit Union Investment Frontier B
(Percentage Composition of Efficient Portfolios)

	1	2	3	4	5	6	7	8	9
A1	2.3	–	–						
A2	–	–	–						
A3	–	–	–						
A4	–	–	0.2						
A5*	–	–	–						
A6*	–	–	–						
A7	68.4	76.1	84.4						
A8	–	–	–						
A9	11.5	5.0	–						
A10	9.9	11.9	12.5						
A11	0.6	0.9	1.0						
A12	–	–	–						
A13	5.9	4.3	–			Infeasible			
A14	1.3	1.3	0.7						
A15	0.1	0.5	1.2						
A16*	–	–	–						
A17*	–	–	–						
A18*	–	–	–						
A19*	–	–	–						
A20*	–	–	–						
A21*	–	–	–						
A22*	–	–	–						
A23*	–	–	–						
A24*	–	–	–						
A25*	–	–	–						
Portfolio return (%)	1.80	1.85	1.90						
Standard deviation (%)	0.13	0.13	0.15						
Shadow price	0.00	0.03	0.09						

Indicates assets excluded from the investment opportunity set.

Table D-11
Credit Union Investment Frontier C
(Percentage Composition of Efficient Portfolios)

	1	2	3	4	5	6	7	8	9
A1	1.0	—	—						
A2	—	—	—						
A3	—	—	—						
A4	—	—	—						
A5*	—	—	—						
A6*	—	—	—						
A7	66.6	76.7	86.2						
A8	—	—	—						
A9	9.4	3.1	—						
A10	10.9	10.7	10.6						
A11	0.5	0.7	0.8						
A12	—	—	—			Infeasible			
A13	6.0	4.2	0.6						
A14	0.8	0.9	0.8						
A15	—	—	0.1						
A16	4.6	3.2	—						
A17	—	—	—						
A18	0.2	0.4	0.8						
A19*	—	—	—						
A20*	—	—	—						
A21*	—	—	—						
A22*	—	—	—						
A23*	—	—	—						
A24*	—	—	—						
A25*	—	—	—						
Portfolio return (%)	1.80	1.85	1.90						
Standard deviation (%)	0.12	0.13	0.14						
Shadow price	0.00	0.03	0.07						

*Indicates assets excluded from the investment opportunity set.

Table D-12
Credit Union Investment Frontier D
(Percentage Composition of Efficient Portfolios)

	1	2	3	4	5	6	7	8	9
A1	–	–	–	–	–		–		
A2	–	–	–	–	–		–		
A3	–	–	–	–	–		–		
A4	–	–	–	–	–		–		
A5*	–	–	–	–	–		–		
A6*	–	–	–	–	–		–		
A7	67.4	75.3	84.3	40.1	–		–		
A8	–	–	–	–	–		–		
A9	5.3	3.3	–	–	–		–		
A10	9.8	11.8	11.8	57.2	92.6	•	80.2	•	•
A11	0.4	0.5	0.3	–	–		–		
A12	–	–	–	–	–		–		
A13	7.4	4.8	1.8	–	–		–		
A14	–	0.8	0.6	–	–		–		
A15	–	–	–	–	–		–		
A16	9.7	3.0	–	–	–		–		
A17	–	–	–	–	–		–		
A18	–	0.3	0.7	–	–		–		
A19*	–	–	–	–	–		–		
A20*	–	–	–	–	–		–		
A21*	–	–	–	–	–		–		
A22*	–	–	–	–	–		–		
A23*	–	–	–	–	–		–		
A24*	–	–	–	–	–		–		
A25	–	0.2	0.4	2.7	7.4		19.8		
Portfolio return (%)	1.80	1.85	1.90	1.95	2.00	2.05	2.10		
Standard deviation (%)	0.11	0.11	0.14	0.25	0.25		1.53		
Shadow price	0.00	0.02	0.06	0.16	0.16		15.50		

*Indicates assets excluded from the investment opportunity set.

Bibliography

Ascheim, J. "Open Market Operations Versus Reserve Requirement Variations." *Economic Journal* 69 (1959):697-704.

Barro, R., and Santomero, A.M. "Household Money Holdings and the Demand Deposit Rate." *Journal of Money, Credit and Banking* 4 (1972):397-413.

Battey, P. "Fed Draft Offers Reserve Interest, Service Fees, Eased Requirements for Demand Deposits." *American Banker*, June 1978, p. 1.

Baughn, W.H., and Walker, C.D., eds. *The Bankers' Handbook*. Homewood, Ill.: Dow-Jones-Irwin, 1966.

Bedford, M.E. "Federal Taxation of Financial Institutions." *Monthly Review*, Federal Reserve Bank of Kansas City, June 1976, pp. 3-15.

Black, F. "Capital Market Equilibrium with Restricted Borrowing." *Journal of Business* 45 (1972):444-455.

_____. "Bank Funds Management in an Efficient Market." *Journal of Financial Economics* 4 (1975):323-339.

Blair, R., and Heggestad, A. "Bank Portfolio Regulation and the Probability of Bank Failure." *Journal of Money, Credit and Banking* 10 (1978):88-93.

Burgess, R.C., and Johnson, K.H. "The Effects of Sampling Fluctuations on the Required Inputs of Security Analysis." *Journal of Financial and Quantitative Analysis* 11 (1976):847-854.

Commission on Financial Structure and Regulation. *Report of the Commission*. Washington, D.C.: Government Printing Office, 1971.

Cozzolino, J., and Taga, T. "On the Separability of Corporate Stockholders' Risk Preference." Mimeographed. Philadelphia, Penn.: University of Pennsylvania, 1976.

Crosse, H. *Management Policies for Commercial Banks*. Englewood Cliffs, N.J.: Prentice-Hall, 1972.

Fama, E.F. *Foundations of Finance*. New York: Basic Books, 1976.

Federal Deposit Insurance Corporation. *Annual Report*. Washington, D.C., various issues.

_____. *Assets and Liabilities of Commercial Banks and Mutual Savings Banks*. Washington, D.C., various issues.

Federal Home Loan Bank Board. *FSLIC-insured Savings and Loan Associations, Combined Financial Statements*. Washington, D.C., various issues.

Federal Reserve Bank of Chicago. *Conference on Bank Structure and Competition*. Chicago: Federal Reserve Bank of Chicago, 1974 and 1975.

Flannery, M.J. *An Economic Evaluation of Credit Unions in the United States*. Boston: Federal Reserve Bank of Boston, Research Report No. 54, 1974.

Grubel, H.G. "Internationally Diversified Portfolio: Welfare Gains and Capital Flow." *American Economic Review* 58 (1968):1299-1314.

Hakanson, N.H. "Mean-Variance Analysis in a Finite World." *Journal of Financial and Quantitative Analysis* 7 (1972):1873-1880.

Hanoch, G., and Levy, H. "The Efficiency Analysis of Choices Involving Risk." *Review of Economic Studies* 36 (1969):335-346.

Hart, O., and Jaffee, D. "On the Application of Portfolio Theory to Depository Financial Intermediaries." *Review of Economic Studies* 41 (1974):129-147.

Hempel, G.H., and Yawitz, J.B. *Financial Management of Financial Institutions.* Englewood Cliffs, N.J.: Prentice-Hall, 1977.

James, J.A. "Portfolio Selection with an Imperfect Competitive Asset Market." *Journal of Financial and Quantitative Analysis* 11 (1976):831-846.

Jessup, P.F., ed. *Innovations in Bank Management.* New York: Holt, Rinehart, and Winston, 1969.

Kane, E.J. "Getting Along Without Regulation Q: Testing the Standard View of Deposit-rate Competition During the 'Wild Card Experiment'." *Journal of Finance* 33 (1978):921-932.

Kendall, M.G., and Stuart, A. *The Advanced Theory of Statistics.* Vol. 2. New York: Hafner Publishing, 1961.

Koehn, M.F., and Santomero, A.M. "Regulation of Bank Capital and Portfolio Risk." Mimeographed. Philadelphia, Penn.: University of Pennsylvania, 1978.

Land, A., and Powell, S. *Fortran Codes for Mathematical Programming: Linear, Quadratic, and Discrete.* New York: Wiley, 1973.

Levy, H., and Sarnat, M. "International Diversification of Investment Portfolios." *American Economic Review* 60 (1970):668-675.

Lintner, J. "The Valuation of Risk Assets and the Selection of Risky Investments in Stock Portfolios and Capital Budgets." *Review of Economics and Statistics* 67 (1965):13-37.

McCall, J.J. "Probabilistic Economics." *Bell Journal of Economics and Management Science* 2 (1971):403-433.

Malinvaud, E. *Lectures on Microeconomic Theory.* Amsterdam: North-Holland Publishing, 1972.

Markowitz, H.M. *Portfolio Selection.* New York: Wiley, 1959.

Mayne, L.S. "The Deposit Reserve Requirement Recommendations of the Commission on Financial Structure and Regulation: An Analysis and Critique." *Journal of Bank Research* 4 (1973):41-51.

Merton, R. "An Analytic Derivation of the Efficient Portfolio Frontier." *Journal of Financial and Quantitative Analysis* 7 (1972):1851-1872.

Michaelsen, J., and Goshay, R. "Portfolio Selection in Financial Intermediaries: A New Approach." *Journal of Financial and Quantitative Analysis* 2 (1967):166-199.

Mossin, J. *Theory of Financial Markets.* Englewood Cliffs, N.J.: Prentice-Hall, 1973.

National Association of Mutual Savings Banks. *National Fact Book of Mutual Savings Banking.* Washington, D.C., various issues.

National Credit Union Administration. *Report of the National Credit Union Administration.* Washington, D.C., various issues.

National Science Foundation. *Evaluation of the Social Impact of Regulation of Consumer Financial Services.* Preliminary Report Prepared by Abt Associates. Cambridge: Abt Associates, Inc., 1977.

Prestopino, C.J. "The Impact of Differential Reserve Requirements on Commercial Bank Liquidity and Portfolio Management." Ph.D. dissertation, University of Pennsylvania, 1974.

Pringle, J. "The Capital Decision in Commerical Banks." *Journal of Finance* 24 (1974):779-796.

Pyle, D.H., and Turnovsky, S.J. "Safety First and Expected Utility Maximization in Mean-Standard Deviation Portfolio Analysis." *Review of Economics and Statistics* 52 (1970):75-81.

Reed, E.W.; Cotter, R.V.; Gill, E.K.; and Smith, R.K. *Commercial Banking.* Englewood Cliffs, N.J.: Prentice-Hall, 1976.

Robichek, A.A.; Cohn, R.; and Pringle, J.J. "Returns on Alternative Investment Media and Implications for Portfolio Construction." *Journal of Business* 45 (1972):427-443.

Robinson, R., and Pettway. *Policies for Optimum Bank Capital.* A Study Prepared for the Trustees of the Banking Research Fund, Association of Reserve City Bankers, 1967.

Roy, A. "Safety First and the Holding of Assets." *Econometrica* 20 (1952):431-449.

Rubinstein, M. "Competition and Approximation." *The Bell Journal of Economics* 9 (1978):280-286.

Santomero, A.M., and Watson, R. "Determining the Optimal Capital Standards for the Banking Industry." *Journal of Finance* 32 (1977):1267-1282.

Sarnat, M.C. "Capital Market Imperfections and the Composition of Optimal Portfolios." *Journal of Finance* 29 (1974):1241-1253.

Scott, K., and Mayer, T. "Risk and Regulation in Banking: Some Proposals for Federal Deposit Insurance Reform." *Stanford Law Review* 23 (1971): 857-902.

Sharpe, W.F. *Portfolio Theory and Capital Markets.* New York: McGraw-Hill, 1970.

Startz, R. "Implicit Interest on Demand Deposits." *Journal of Monetary Economics*, in press.

The First Boston Corporation. *Handbook of Securities of the U.S. Government and Federal Agencies.* 27th ed. New York: The First Boston Corporation, 1976.

Tobin, J. "Liquidity Preferences and Behavior Towards Risk." *Review of Economic Studies* 25 (1958):65-85.

Tsiang, S.C. "The Rationale of the Mean-Standard Deviation Analysis, Skewness Preference, and the Demand for Money." *American Economic Review* 62 (1972):354-371.

U.S. League of Savings Associations. *Savings and Loan Fact Book.* Chicago, various issues.

U.S. Senate Committee on Banking, Housing, and Urban Affairs. *Compendium of Major Issues in Banking.* Washington, D.C., 1975.

Vojta, G. *Bank Capital Adequacy.* New York: Citicorp, 1973.

Wallich, H. "Some Thoughts on Capital Adequacy." Speech delivered in Washington, D.C., February 1975.

Watson, R. "Insuring Some Progress in the Bank Capital Hassle." *Business Review*, Federal Reserve Bank of Philadelphia, July/August 1974, pp. 3-19.

Index

About the Author

Michael F. Koehn is a financial economist at Arthur D. Little, Inc., where he specializes in the economics of regulated industries and financial intermediaries. His recent work is in the theory and application of alternative rate-making systems for regulated industries and the effects of regulation on the risk-return characteristics of the firm.

Dr. Koehn received the A.B. and A.M. degrees in economics from the University of California, Irvine, and the University of Chicago, respectively. He received the Ph.D. degree in finance from the Wharton School of the University of Pennsylvania. While at the University of Pennsylvania, Dr. Koehn was senior research analyst at the Wharton Applied Research Center.